'Cos That's The Way It Is

A Mother's Eye View of
Wartime Barrow

By

Lilian Wookey
www.wookeysworld.com

Books available in this series:

'Cos That's The Way It Was:
A Child's Eye View of Wartime Barrow

'Cos That's The Way It Is:
A Mother's Eye View of Wartime Barrow

DEDICATION

Dedicated to the many ordinary, working-class mothers, sisters and daughters who were left behind to cope alone after their men enlisted in the British Armed Forces during World War II (1939-1945).

CONTENTS

SUPPORTING PHOTOS

ACKNOWLEDGEMENTS

With special thanks to Jeanette for all her help in the initial editing & publication of the very first edition of this book and for her continuous support.

Additional thanks to Caroline of *PC-Magic (Furness)* for her help with all things computer and 'techie', as well her invaluable assistance in the re-editing and hard copy publication of the second edition of the book.

Thank you too, to all the women who have shared their stories with me. These I have amalgamated into this book, especially those of Mrs Clark and Lillian Baines.

I would also like to thank my many friends for the support and the confidence they have given to me when writing this story.

This story is made up of true stories I have heard, seen and been told about. It is written as a Novella.

"Friends are the jewels in life's crown"

Lilian Wookey

**"Mists of memories swirl through our aged minds.
Fragile bodies deny our robust history".**

Lilian Wookey

PROLOGUE

This story is set during WWII in an industrial shipbuilding town in the north-west of England. It is the story of wartime from an ordinary working class wife-and-mother's point of view and starts in the year 1940 when Elizabeth is 26 years old and married to Fred. They have two small children called Tom and Jane.

Elizabeth lives with her small family in a terraced house, which was originally purpose-built to house the workers of the local shipyard. Her husband Fred has a responsible job in the town's local paper mill, and serves as a part-time fireman; both are very good jobs and means they are slightly better off than most of their neighbours.

Elizabeth is a very good manager. She cooks, sews, knits, and keeps her house spotlessly clean. However, her marriage is not as happy as it perhaps could be, mainly because Fred is possessive. She married her husband – who is six years her senior - when she was only 18 years old, he was her very first boyfriend and she believes he deliberately made her pregnant. She resents having to be a wife and mother so early in her young life, she's always wanted to work but he won't allow it. He is very jealous of her and always worries she will leave him for someone else.

In 1939, all men aged 20-21 were compulsorily drafted into the British Armed Forces and two of Fred's brothers were called up. Although Fred works in a reserved occupation as a fireman, early in 1941 and completely out of the blue he volunteers for the army alongside his brothers. He takes a drastic drop in wage, and Elizabeth has to start work in order to support her small family.

Starting from the great snowfall and freeze in the winter of 1940-41, her life changes forever. She finds she loves working and starts a completely new life.

"Please tell me you'll love and stay with me for the rest of my life?"

I know I can't promise that, not yet. "I love you, will always, and forever". I reply, kissing him passionately.

He responds as I knew he would, and I feel a passion rising in me that I have never felt before. We make love again and it is heaven. He kisses my eyes, lips, neck then my breasts. He strokes and explores every part of my body. I realise I am encountering new heights and feelings that I've never experienced before. I hold him as close as I can, want him to swallow me up, engulf me, so that we are never parted. Then I feel as if fireworks are exploding through my body and I never want it to stop. But it does, and I fall back into his arms. This time we lay together in total exhaustion. I am so content. I think about my feelings for him and know I cannot ignore them.

CHAPTER ONE:
HARD TIMES

We women are finding life the hardest. Even though the snow has now gone, it's still a struggle and we've lost old friends and neighbours, like Mrs Platt. Her heart was broken after receiving those two telegrams. Who would have thought her only two boys would be killed, and in such a short space of time? How can our lives ever be normal again? It doesn't bear thinking about. I am so frightened. What if we lose this war?

I sip my tea as I sit there, thinking. Even though I know I'm one of the lucky ones, life's still hard and miserable. Fred's exempt because of his work so hasn't been called up to enlist for the forces. He earns decent money at the paper mill and he's also on-call most nights with the fire service.

Figure 2 - Barrow Fire Station with Fire Engines

Nevertheless, the everyday grind of finding enough food to feed our small family is tough. The worst part of life for us women are the queues. Sometimes you only get a couple of carrots or perhaps an onion, and that is if you're lucky. So as a family, we are very fortunate because we have our allotment and the hens. Also, Mother closed her small grocer's shop the day WWII was declared; she remembered how awful WWI had been for everyone. There were thousands of poor families with nothing at all to fall back on, and Mother did worry about closing so suddenly, feeling selfish for just thinking of her own family. Still, it was a rented shop so she immediately gave one week's notice and left.

We used to live in Arthur Street. However, since Mother made a bit of spare cash with her shop, she could afford to pay a higher rent. So we moved onto Rawlinson Street which wasn't too far away but classed as a better neighbourhood, Mother always wanted to better herself for our sakes although she has many good friends in that street. But these are hard times, some families are really large and the kids run wild. Their poor mothers are ground down just trying to feed them, and that's mostly with bread and potatoes. Even the comedians who come to *His Majesty's Theatre* make jokes about Arthur Street. Some of them are funny - but not if you live there. One of the jokes told is, "They are so dirty, they keep a pig in the corner as an air freshener", another is that "the kids play tig with axes". Mother hates the way they tear the street to pieces like this. Many have spotless houses and most of the kids, though poor, know how to behave. Nevertheless, she moved out as quickly as she could.

Selfish or not, times are hard and I don't care – family *should* come first. I've told Mother to hide what she's saved because we all know Dad will steal it to pay his gambling debts; he sells everything he can get his hands on.

Mother's passed a lot of tea, sugar, cans of food and a large double biscuit tin full of rice to me and my sister Nellie. Our Bella's still at home and she gets the best of everything, spoilt rotten she is! We hope the rice will last as long as this damned war does. It's more than a year and a half since it started; no-one thought it would last more than two years. I think we were all wrong. Food is getting scarce, and the extras won't last much longer. The ration of 2oz of tea a week hasn't gone anywhere. Even the additional packets I've had off Mother are already finished.

I jump as I hear the backyard door bang. I've been so busy just sitting and thinking about things that I didn't hear her open it. I wait.

The scullery door flies back with a bang and she comes rushing in. It'll be "Mam this and Mam that", all she wants is my attention; she's hard work. Thank God Tom gives me some peace.

I sigh. "Go back and close the door, Jane".

"But Mam, Tom'll be here soon". She has to argue. I push her back towards the door. She's a lazy madam, always has to have the last word.

"Tom isn't your servant, do as you're told or you'll get a slap".

She whines as usual, "Orrrrrr, Mammm---".

I point my finger at the door, "Now!"

I'd thought it was bad enough having to get married at 18. Still, my Tom was such a good baby but Jane is a different kettle of fish. Demanding from the start, I had a terrible time with her. She came as a breech birth. Took hours! The midwife was with me from two in the morning until Fred had to go and knock Dr Merrill up to help deliver her. It meant he'd had to get out of bed at 5.30am and he wasn't happy, probably had a skin full before he went to bed; they say he can drink a whole bottle of whisky in one night.

Nearly killed me, Jane did. Must have known I didn't want another baby. It was hard on the midwife too, I was a bit sorry for her. I decided there and then that she wouldn't be coming here again. Dot, the lass next door, had had her baby at around 12.30am the same night. The midwife had been with her all that day and night so I'm sure she was exhausted. Dot was lucky – she'd had another baby boy. I know *I* would have been a lot happier with another lad like our Tom. Even feeding Jane was a problem that drove me mad. Then the nurse found that Jane was tongue-tied and snipped beneath her tongue, but I still had no sleep for ages.

Fred had always wanted me to get pregnant again, and I tried everything not to. Mother told me to use a piece of sponge tied on a long piece of ribbon or string, which worked for some time. Then, just once, when Fred came home from work, he had a treat for me. He'd been for his usual teatime pint with his mates and he brought me half a pint of Guinness home in his Billy can. He knew the kids were at their Nana's for tea, and it was nice, just the two of us. We had our meal and I had my Guinness which made me feel very mellow. He insisted, and I gave in that one time without thinking. You know how it is!

When I first realised I might be pregnant, I drank a full bottle of gin. Unsurprisingly, it didn't work and I was sick for hours afterwards, my head so bad I thought I was dying. The next things I tried were a very hot bath and jumping off the kitchen table; they didn't work either! I even thought of finding a backstreet abortionist. Then I remembered my school friend Audrey whose mam had taken her to one when she was 16; she'd ended up bleeding to death. Thankfully, the woman who performed the abortion went to prison.

I know it's selfish but I really don't want to be tied to my home day after day, and Jane is so demanding! Maybe it is a modern idea in this age to want a job when you're married with children, but it's what I need; it *is* nearly 1941 after all. A lot more women are working these days because their husbands have been called up but Fred won't hear of it, he's so old fashioned.

I sit there thinking of when I met Fred for the first time. Was it really only ten years ago? I'd seen him in the park on my previous month's Sunday off and thought he'd seemed really nice. To me, he was the most handsome boy I'd ever seen. He had thick, wavy dark hair, deep brown eyes and was tall, slim and broad-shouldered. I thought about him often during that next long month. I just couldn't wait for Sarah and me to do our parade around the park again the next Sunday I was home. I spent sleepless nights worrying he wouldn't be there or would have a girlfriend on his arm.

They kept me very busy at the big house where I worked, and it was usually around 7 or 8pm until I finished all my jobs, despite only supposedly being on call from 6am until 6pm. Because I finished so late I was usually exhausted, so tired I would doze off whilst eating my meal. I normally couldn't wait to get into my bed, falling asleep almost immediately. However after that first time I met Fred, my routine was different and I would lie awake for hours thinking about seeing him on my next Sunday off.

They called me an 'assistant lady's maid' because I looked after Miss Anna. She was one year younger than me. As I was in training,

I only looked after her fully one day a month when the 'proper' lady's maid took her day off. I felt very lucky to have this position as I would be able to progress when Miss Anna's lady's maid retired (she was quite old - about 45 years - that's even older than my Mother).

There were many girls like myself applying for the position. I left school as soon as I was 14 years old and was with the family for two years. It was like I seemed to leave school one day and start work the next (although I did have a couple of days off to get my things together). Luckily Madam Greenhill at the big house chose me. I was very tidily dressed when I went for the interview. Some of the other girls seemed poorly dressed and slightly grubby. Although I was sorry for them, I was glad to be the one who got the position. Mother had made sure I looked nice for my interview. Moreover, because she'd been so well brought up herself, she'd taught us to speak well and respectfully.

As I was only training, every morning I lit the fires in the sitting room, dining room and my young lady's bedroom. Then I'd have to help Cook to prepare the breakfasts. I would take Miss Anna's breakfast tray to her bedroom door where her lady's maid would take the tray from me. I'd prepared it myself and taken it to her room but her maid wouldn't let me in. I didn't know why but she was quite snooty with me.

I realise with a start that I should stop daydreaming and set the table for tea. Fred's a much better earner than many of the husbands in our street. He's bossy like the rest though, insisting his meal is on the table as he walks through the door.

When I've finished laying the table, I sit down again sipping my tea, still thinking about the last ten years. I was only 16 when I met Fred, it now seems so very long ago. Even if things had gone in another direction, I still think I would have married him. Nevertheless, I would have liked to have made up my own mind as to whether we should have had children - at least, so quickly. I think of how happy I was to meet him; I was so in love at that time. Again, my mind wanders back to those times.

At last, it's my Sunday off, and I help Mother to make Sunday dinner. Then sit down to eat with her, Dad and my sisters Nellie and Bella. Afterwards, I'm allowed to go out to meet my friend Sarah as she makes the other two do the washing up.

I can't wait to get to the park. I'm wearing a pretty new blouse that Mother has made for me out of a cream cotton sheet she'd kept for best but had decided it's more useful as a couple of blouses for me and my sister Nellie, who's also started to work. There are only 11 months between us so people used to think we were twins, although she is tinier and fairer than me. Now we have both grown up, I think she is quite fragile so I try to take care of her. Bella, our youngest sister, is a different kettle of fish and is quite sassy!

Now Bella's annoyed because she didn't get a blouse – but she's still at school whereas Nellie and I are able to give Mother some money for housekeeping every month now, and Mother wants us to be as well dressed as possible. Bella sulks as usual and Mother tells her off, saying she's a 'stroppy little madam' and that we are now bringing money in to put food on the table. Bella's 12 next month and doesn't know how lucky she is.

Dad unfortunately lost his hearing during the first world war and hadn't been able to find a job he could do since. He's lucky really because many men were blinded by gas during the war and subsequently became very depressed. Their families had a very hard time as there was very little help for them. Many a family was broken up and had to go into the Workhouse.

So Dad does some wheeling and dealing. I think he takes money off other gamblers when he wins a cycling race, Mother gets a bit off him before the bookie sees it, assuming she finds out in time! I don't know how she does it but she seems to have a spy in the bookies. I've heard her tell him he won't get his oats if he doesn't cough up and that seems to work. She says Dad would bet on two flies crawling up the wall to see which one was the fastest!

Now that Nellie and me are working, our family is on Easy Street compared to how it used to be for us. I don't know how Mother ever managed! She still buys and sells bits and pieces to make extra money here and there, and I'm sure she used to go without food as she never used to sit down for a meal when we all did, always saying she'd eaten already. Now I've noticed she eats with us more and enjoys her food. She's only about 4'11" tall and is getting quite plump. It suits her.

Today, I have set my hair into the fashionable Marcel waves and worn my pretty brown cloche hat to go out. It's the first new thing I've bought with the pocket money Mother's been able to give me out of my wages. I feel really smart but hope no-one notices my well-worn shoes. I'm saving up for a new pair which I hope I can buy next month.

We have just done our first turn around the park without seeing the boys and I've started to feel a bit fed up. There are so many boys and girls doing the same thing, all walking around the park in their Sunday best; Mother calls it the 'Sunday Parade'. I'm not interested in any of the other boys who try to catch our attention, and Sarah digs me as we walk along, "You're so boring, I know who you're looking for. Why don't we stop to talk to some of the others?" she complains.

We start to walk down the Cenotaph steps as I protest "I'm not looking for anyone", but I know I'm fibbing, not that I was going to admit it to her! She'll tell him right away if we do meet them. Abruptly, Sarah pokes me in the side, "You're in luck kid, here they are".

Figure 3 - Steps Leading Down from the Cenataph

He and the other boy - who I know is called Ken because Sarah knows him - are walking up the steps towards us. They both have their sports' coats thrown casually over their shoulders, and are smoking and laughing. They look like they own life itself. They smile at us, making it obvious they like us as we pass by. My friend Sarah is much bolder than me so she smiles back at them whereas I just blush and giggle a bit. She fancies Ken, the other boy, a lot.

"Come ON", she says after we pass them. Setting a fast pace, it's clear she wants to almost run right around the lake back to the steps so we can pass them again!

"Sarah, slow up!", I puff. I'm already hot and bothered at seeing him again and don't want to get there all sweaty. Sarah is my best friend but she embarrasses me all the time; we are so different. Because I'm only 16, I haven't had a boyfriend yet but Sarah's 17 and has had a couple already. Mother keeps telling me she's fast and she hopes she keeps her hand on her penny, but I'm not too sure what she means. Mother says to me, "Don't forget I've tried to bring you up properly". I'm not sure what difference that makes either but I know I'm much shyer than Sarah.

We are getting near to where we should be passing the boys again, at the bottom of the long flight of steps going up to the Cenotaph. We set off, casually walking slowly up and then, there they are walking down towards us. Sarah digs me and whispers, "We have timed it well!" We slowly pass each other, and they both stop and smile. Sarah laughs and pushes me into Ken, the boy she likes.

I am mortified. "Stop it!" I tell her off and can feel my face blushing. "Sorry", I say. I can't think of anything else to say.

Sarah just stands there giggling, "Hey butcher boy, I know you", she says.

"I know you too, you come in to get half a pound of mince for ya Ma and I always give you a bit extra", he laughs back at her.

Sarah flirts with him and laughing aloud, she says, "Why d'ya think mi Mam sends me? She's not daft ya know". I am just standing there, still blushing whilst his friend stares at me, making me feel even more embarrassed.

"I'm Sarah, what's your name, butcher boy?". As if she doesn't know! Sarah's behaving fast as Mother says she does.

"I'm Ken and this is my pal Fred. He likes you". I think he and Fred are looking at me though Fred says nothing.

Sarah laughs again, "Do you mean ME?" This time it's Fred who looks embarrassed, "No, I like your friend", he says as he looks at me again. I shiver with excitement at knowing he has chosen me. Knowing I'd already chosen him on my last Sunday afternoon parade. The only thing is, because I'm in service at the big house in the country, I only have the one Sunday a month off. What boy will want to wait for me?

Sarah won't behave, "Why, what's wrong with me?" She stares at him all straight-faced like.

He starts to stutter, "Um, a-ah, well now't really, but I do like your friend".

Sarah laughs again, "Aye lad, don't get so worried, I was only joshing thi'. It's butcher boy I'm interested in. Lizzie is her name". She goes over to Ken and links his arm. "Wanta watch the band?" she asks as she walks down the steps to the bandstand with him.

Now it's my turn to almost stutter! "My name's Elizabeth. My Mother would kill anyone who calls me Lizzie and Sarah knows that".

She turns and laughs again, "Why does it matter? Or are you already planning to take him home to meet the parents?"

"Stop it Sarah, you're embarrassing me", I'm practically spluttering which is definitely not the way to impress. Sarah though, is waltzing off by now.

She turns around as they leave and says, "You're so old fashioned, Liz".

Fred and me trail along behind them like two lost souls. I try to think of something to say but nothing is forthcoming. As we make our way towards our beautiful Victorian bandstand, our fingers accidentally touch. I move mine as fast as he moves his. Well, I think, he doesn't fancy me enough to try to hold my hand.

Sarah has found a space amongst the throng of people on the grass by the bandstand. They are all watching and listening to our really great Town Band who are all dressed up in their Sunday Best maroon and black uniforms. They are playing tunes from the musicals that are on at the pictures now. Sarah has flung herself down on the patch of grass pulling Ken down beside her. She's not let go of his hand once. I sit down beside them and Fred starts to sit down beside me.

"Here, sit on my jacket". He straightens the jacket he's been carrying and I slide onto it. It means we are sitting very close together and I find I kind of like that - although I still can't think of anything to say. The silence is only broken by Sarah's giggling. I decide I have to say something so turn my head and at the same time he decides to talk to me. Our faces almost collide and I'm so close I can smell the cigarettes on his breath.

He says, "Sorry".

"You didn't do anything" I manage to get out. And then he kisses me.

"Now I have! S-o-r-r-y". He kisses me in between each letter, then looks straight into my eyes, "You do realise you are beautiful?"

Me, beautiful? I can feel myself blushing again, I hate it! I'm sure my nose swells and I look anything but beautiful. I pull away turning my face so he won't notice. Now he is really sorry and worried.

"Elizabeth, have I said something wrong?"

I finally turn around and look at him, "No, I'm just not used to what boys say".

He laughs, "I'm a man, not a boy. I'm in my twenties and have a decent job, it's a while since I was a boy. I really like you Elizabeth, and wonder if you could like me enough to go out with me?"

I nod. How can I tell him that's exactly what I want? I'm not sure what Dad will think about it.

He kisses me gently, "Does a nod mean 'yes' Elizabeth?", he asks quietly. I nod again. Oh heck, Sarah has noticed.

"What are you two up to then?" She says quite loudly.

"Shush, Sarah, people are looking at us," I plead.

She laughs, "Come on. Spill it".

Fred smiles at her and says quietly, "Elizabeth has agreed to go out with me".

This makes her louder, "Oh my God, that was quick work! Although she's had a thing for you for quite some time".

"Oh Sarah, shush", my face flames again.

Fred holds my hand and says, "I couldn't be happier, Elizabeth".

Suddenly pulling myself together out of my daydream, I look at the clock to see the time. I realise I will have to rush to get the meal into the oven. I go into the scullery and turn on the oven to heat up, then put both the shepherd's pie and the rice pudding I've prepared into it. I make myself a fresh pot of tea, take it into the kitchen and sit back down at the table again. I leave the tea to mash for a minute then pour myself a cup. Sipping it, I stare into space, allowing myself to drift back into my thoughts of the past again.

Once I had started to see Fred, we were considered to be courting and the next two years flew by. I saw Fred on all my monthly Sundays off and we got engaged. I smile to myself as I think about that special time.

Our engagement is a lovely day. Mother and Dad let me invite Sarah and Ken to tea. I know Dad doesn't approve of Sarah much but she is my best friend. Our Bella is working now and hasn't had to leave home. She works in a dress shop so really thinks she's 'it' and is still a little madam. Today though, I love her. She and our Nellie have bought us an engagement present! A pair of lovely, handmade, fine cotton pillowcases, beautifully crocheted around the edges. This precious piece of linen is the start of my bottom drawer.

I don't know how Mother manages her housekeeping because Dad still spends most of his money on gambling. He even tried to borrow a bob off me when he saw Mother give me pocket money from my wages. That's nearly all I have for the month. Not that I need any money at the big house except for the bus fare to get up there and come home again. Mother would have given Dad a right telling off if she'd known. I didn't tell her but I didn't give it to him either. I did however feel so mean I gave him a penny instead.

On the day of our engagement celebration, we have a lovely ham and salad tea and Mother lets me make a Victoria sponge cake.

By now I've passed my 18th birthday. Sarah is 19, almost 20. She and Ken have set a wedding date and I'm to be bridesmaid. I'm almost as excited as she is! I'm not in a rush to get married myself though. I know most of the girls around here seem to think they're going to be left on the shelf if they aren't married by 20, and I know Fred wants us to marry even sooner than that. He's getting frustrated because I won't let him make love to me but I really know Dad would kill me if I became pregnant.

Then everything changes. The last Sunday I was having off from the big house altered everything. I was ready with my coat and hat to catch my bus home when I remembered something. I crept down to the larder in the kitchen and sneaked out a freshly baked loaf of bread. I picked up the bread knife and started to saw off a large piece. I always take Mother a piece with thick butter on it. I know I shouldn't but it's a real treat for her and she loves it. This time however, the kitchen door swung open and Cook walked in. She saw what I was up to and barked, "What are you doing?"

I jumped so hard, the knife slipped and cut my hand rather badly. I couldn't hide it. "Sorry, sorry". I attempted to hide my hand but there was blood everywhere.

"Here". Cook passed me a kitchen towel, "Wrap it up".

"Thank you, I was just taking Mother some of your delicious bread", I whispered.

"Don't thank me. You were stealing. I would report you upstairs if you hadn't made such a mess of your hand. I think God has already passed judgment so I will merely dismiss you. You could have gone to court for this. Go and pack, then you leave. I think you're a very lucky girl that I am such a Christian woman".

"Thank you Cook", I said, red-faced as I left the kitchen. As I rush to pack, my thoughts are so jumbled. I don't know what I am going to do now, Mother depends on my wage. How am I going to tell Fred what I have done? He'll probably finish with me when I admit I have been stealing.

It's later in the day and Fred's coming to pick me up to go for a walk. Dad and Mother really like him and they both think I'm very lucky to meet such a hardworking man. I talk to Mother before he comes, "Please don't let Dad mention what's happened. I want to tell Fred myself".

"You'll have to tell your Dad to say nothing, you know what he's like". She shakes her head at me.

"Please", I plead again, "Tell him I have to explain and that Fred might finish with me. I want to do it privately".

"OK", she says. "I know how much your Dad wants you to settle down with him. I'll warn him that if he comes out with it like a bull in a china shop, he'll ruin everything". I think I've probably already ruined everything anyway.

When Fred arrives, Mother always makes him a cup of tea as I'm usually faffing about, finishing getting ready to go out with him. Today though I'm ready and only have to put on my gloves so that I can cover my bandage. I went to the hospital when I arrived home and had to have three stitches. When I walk into the parlour all ready to go out, Fred's surprised and says, "I'll just finish my tea;

I've something I want to ask your Dad and Mam". I can't think what he's going to ask! He'd already asked them if he could marry me.

Today, he asks them if I can go to Blackpool with him and stay overnight on my next Sunday off. Two of his sisters and their husbands were also going. I'm quite shocked. I had been away for the day with him last year but it was with Mother, Dad and my sisters. I look at Mother who's looking at Dad. He's so deaf and it's obvious he hasn't heard what Fred asked. Mother's already told Dad not to say anything about my being sacked. I cringe, waiting for his answer as she explains to him what Fred had said.

He says in his very loud voice, whilst looking at me, "Aye lad you can, once she has told you".

Fred looks at me, confused, "What does he mean?"

I stand up, "I have to talk to you". I walk up the lobby so he has to follow me. "Let's go for a walk up the Abbey, it's quiet there and I have something serious to tell you".

He looks shocked and worried. "What is it?"

"Please let's walk a while, I'll explain then", I reply, sadly.

I make sure I walk beside him so that he has to hold my right hand. I really don't want to tell him yet. I even make sure we walk on the right so that he is on the side to the road. Men always walk that way with a woman so that she's protected from getting water or mud splashed onto her. If we had walked on the other side, he would have insisted on changing hands, and then would have realised that I had a dressing on my hand and I would have had to explain myself. We walk and walk in silence, every time he tries to ask me I shake my head. Finally, the ruins of the Furness Abbey come into sight and as there's no-one else around, I tearfully confess. He grabs me and holds me tight, I can feel him trembling as my head nestles into his chest. I know it, he's so shocked at what I have done, he can't bear to speak to me.

He pushes me away and I look up at him. But he's laughing, fit to bust. "How can you think something like that would make any difference to how I feel about you?"

I'm so surprised I whisper, "I stole and was sacked".

He put a finger to my mouth. "A slice of bread for your Mam and then her telling you it was an act of God, I wish I could tell her what I think. If times weren't so hard, you wouldn't have been working like a slave in that house. I think it's time we were married, don't you?"

I'm not sure so I don't say anything. He looks surprised. I know he's reliable but he is the first boyfriend I have had and is very possessive. I know I have to say something so I say, "Let's go on the weekend before we decide a date". I realise I need time to think.

So we had our weekend with separate rooms as Dad said we had to. That was when two things happened that were to change my life forever: Fred came to my room that night, and we made love for the first time. He promised he would be careful. Which was when I found out promises aren't always kept.

I've been home from the big house three months now. Mother wasn't as shocked as I thought she would be when I lost that job. I don't know what Cook told Madam Greenhill but I received the wages for the days I'd worked in the last month. That gave Mother the extra money that would at least last for the next month. Luckily, Mother had a friend who worked in the local laundry and had found out they were looking for staff the week after I arrived home. Mother took me to see her and recommended me, and I started work the very next week. The laundry is hard and heavy work but I realise how lucky I am to have found another job so quickly. I stand at a press for nine hours a day, with half an hour for dinner. It's so hot and I start to be sick every day. After three months, I feel quite ill and have lost a lot of weight so Mother makes me an appointment to see the Doctor.

I was married to Fred the next month, April 1932.

Now I feel sad as I think about my wedding day, though it was everything I had dreamt of. I wore my Mother's wedding dress, a beautiful cream satin, the kind of dress I could never have been able to afford to buy, and it fit me like glove. Except for the length that is, it was a little short because Mother is at least 3" shorter than I am. Auntie Florrie, Mother's sister, was a seamstress so added a beautiful old piece of cream lace around the hem as a wedding present. It was perfect. Although I was over three months pregnant, I'd lost so much weight that it didn't show.

I felt sorry for Mother when I put the wonderful gown on, knowing how much her life had changed after she married Dad. She hadn't told any of us that she'd kept the dress as Dad would have sold it to settle his gambling debts if he'd *got his hands on it! But another two years later, our Nellie was also married in it. Mother finally sold it herself, and because of the war and the shortages it caused, she was glad of the money. Her friend had told her that the daughter of a very well off family she was currently working for was getting married, and that they wanted a special dress for her. So Mother showed her friend her dress; she loved it and told her employers. They arranged to view the dress when Dad was out, and absolutely loved it! Mother nearly fainted at the amount of money they offered but only if they could buy it at once. She sold it there and then! She was pleased it was going to a home where she was sure it would be well loved. It was such a large amount of money that she was able to add to the little stash of savings she'd hidden from Dad, resulting in having enough to buy our house from the landlord. She never told Dad though, he thought they were still renting.*

I had stars in my eyes in those days. On my wedding day, I thought that I was the luckiest girl in the world. Fred looked so handsome in his black suit and white wing-collared shirt. He'd grown a moustache for a few months before as it had become very fashionable, and he looked grand. The day we married, I felt like a queen. Afterwards, we had a small tea for the family at Mother and Dad's house. Then we left for our new home - we couldn't afford a honeymoon. Still, we were lucky because most working class, newly married couples had to live with family for the first few years. But Fred had managed to get us a rented house just around the corner from my Mother and Dad.

When Fred opened the front door of our new home, he swung me up into his arms and carried me over the threshold. Then putting me down, he placed a record on the gramophone he'd bought when he first started work. He then walked over to me, held his hand out and we danced to 'Just the Way You Look Tonight'. I felt we were dancing just like Fred Astaire and Ginger Rogers did in the film. It was a very special moment in our lives, a moment I'll never forget.

I hear her bang the yard door and rush in like a whirlwind. "Mam I'm 'ungry, I want mi tea!". I realise I've been dreaming of times that were really good for me but which have now changed. Her demands bring me back to reality. "You can wait 'til Tom and Dad's home", I tell her.

CHAPTER TWO:
HE'S ENLISTED

How *could* he enlist? His job prevented him being called up so he's enlisted voluntarily.

I'd just come into the scullery after hanging out the washing and was thinking to myself. The only time I enjoy Mondays are when my sheets and towels are pegged on the washing line. They are so white they glow.

As I go through the door into the kitchen, I look at my hands. I hate them. They're very rough and red from the all the washing and scrubbing. And I still have to scrub the flagstones in the scullery. I sit at the kitchen table and rub Vaseline into them to help the cracks heal. I know it's good for them but when I see the adverts for real handcream in the *Ladies Journal*, I very much wish I could afford it. Of course, most women who can afford it don't do their own washing! I remember when I worked in the laundry, people even sent their vests and knickers in for us to launder. Some of them were not very nice either.

I decide I need a cuppa. As I put the kettle on, the front door's knocked really hard and I nearly jump out of my skin, almost dropping the teapot. I know it's not family or friends because nobody ever knocks and waits. My front door's always unlocked so after a quick tap, they just open it and walk in. In fact, I don't know of many people around here who do lock their doors.

Rushing up the lobby, I feel afraid of what I'm going to find on the other side of the door. I open it carefully to find the telegram boy standing there. He hands me the piece of paper he's holding and it's all I can do to take the damned telegram off him. I sign his paper and he pedals away as fast as he can. It must be hard for the poor lad - telegrams are nearly always bad news now. Closing the door, I lean against the lobby wall and open the telegram, despite it being addressed to Fred and my having never opened anything addressed to him before. I assume it must be about one of his brothers as they are all in the army now. Of course, common sense should have told me a telegram of that nature would have gone to his mother.

Unsurprisingly, it isn't about either of his brothers.

I read through the telegram again and again, and cannot believe what I'm reading. I hear a strange noise and realise it's me howling. How *could* he? I feel as though he has stamped on my heart. Then I become angry; to do *this*, to us, his family. I go back into the kitchen and sit down, re-reading the telegram over and over. Jane's heard me crying and rushes in from the backstreet, wanting to know what the matter is and as usual, tries to climb up to sit on my knee. I push her away but she's so upset I finally let her up onto my lap. The front door bangs open and Mrs Carr rushes in, shocked at the noise. I wave the paper at her and say, "Telegram".

"What's the matter, lass? You were making so much noise I thought you were being murdered, eeee I don't know..." she starts to say.

"Don't know? You *don't know?*" I realise I'm being rude and she doesn't deserve it. I pass her the telegram.

She reads it once, then again, and says, "Now then 'Lizbeth, don't take on so much. There might be an explanation. You'll have to wait 'til he gets home".

She jumps up, hugs me then says, "I have to get back. Listen to my lot, you can hear them through t'wall. Sounds like they're killing each other. Dad's not home from work yet. Gonna have to go. Kill 'em mi'self I will! You need your Mam. Can take Jane wi' me if you want?"

"My Mother? No she's the last one I want here". I know I am snapping at her.

"OK get your coat Jane, you're coming win' me".

Of course, Jane cries, "No I want to stay with mi mam".

As she clings to me, I tell Mrs Carr, "She'll be too much trouble. I know how she is. Our Tom will be upset as well when he gets in from school. I want Fred to see what he has done to them and to me".

Mrs Carr leaves and although I asked her not to, she still sends one of her boys with a message asking Mother to come round right away. As usual, my friend ignores me. However, she was right this time. Mother turns up immediately and although I'm glad to see her, I know she can't help me out this time. Anyway she thinks the sun shines out of Fred's backside. But even she realises how hard this is going to be for all of us.

I need an explanation from him, my mind's swirling. Just wait until he comes home from work! How does he think we are going to survive, his wage will be less than half it is now? He's never let me go out to work since we married. Not because of his pride but his jealousy and possessiveness. He thinks I would meet another fella who would take me away from him. I always thought his reasons for being so jealous were because of his mother running off. She left him and siblings behind in Liverpool when he was young.

I sip the cup of tea Mother made before she left. I'm crying again, thinking about our life and how his earlier years have spoiled so much of the time we've spent together. How could his mother do it, leaving her kids with a drunken dad? They'd had to fend for themselves and as Fred was the oldest, he must have had to take the brunt of the problems. I know he's had really hard and bad times. Still, all the kids finally forgave her, including Fred. So why take it out on me? When they all finally did live together again, they easily accepted their new stepfather as well as the others who were their half-brothers and sisters, and Fred was always the 'big brother'. He's never told me of these things, I've gathered bits and pieces about their early lives and put two and two together. Now I think about all the stories I've heard from his sisters over the years.

They were left on their own with their irresponsible and drunken father. Their mother had recently let them know where she was living, and the older boys decided they had to get to her somehow. Fred's oldest sister Margaret was 15, his other sister Fay 11, so they had to pay for their train fares. They were able to take the two younger boys for free because they were quite small in stature - Margaret had told the ticket collector they were both under three years old. She warned James (who was just four) and Robert (nearly five) that they had to be three on the train.

Fred and his brothers had literally begged, stolen, borrowed and pleaded to get enough money together for the train fare so that the two girls and the two boys could travel in safety to their new home.

Margaret had laughed as she told me how James had nearly dropped them all into trouble. A nice woman on the train had given the two small boys a piece of cake each and James had offered his sisters a bite of his. The woman was so impressed with his kindness that she gave the two girls a piece each as well.

She said to James, "What a kind little boy you are, how old are you?"

James answered truthfully, "I'm three on the train but four when I get off!"

Margaret explained very quickly, "We're going to find our mother and only had the money for us two girls".

The woman seemed shocked and looked as if she was going to cry. "Listen, love", she said, "You don't have to worry, I won't say anything". From then on, she shared her food with them and acted as if they were with her when the ticket inspector passed through. She left the train a couple of stops before them, giving Margaret a shilling to get some chips for them all when they got off the train.

"See", Margaret had said to me, "There are a lot of good people in the world".

It used to break my heart hearing other stories of the life they had lived in Liverpool. It was mainly from his sisters because Fred never told me anything unless we were all together having a drink. I found out that Fred and his two other brothers had cycled all the way up from Liverpool even though they were only in their very early teens. Their sisters told me it had taken them nearly three days to get there on their old bicycles. The journey was around 100 miles! They'd slept in the hedgerows and had had to steal six eggs from a henhouse because nothing was left after they'd eaten the little bread they'd taken with them. They'd had nothing to cook the eggs in though so they'd swallowed them raw. They were practically starving by the time they arrived at their new home.

Fred never talked to me about any of this and became angry if I asked him. The only time he ever talked about his real dad in front of me was when his sister and husband came to visit on my birthday. We'd all had a couple of drinks and she told me their dad had been tough. Fred agreed and they laughed together when she asked him if he remembered the night their dad had come home covered in blood. This is when I finally realised how hard their lives had been.

Fred's dad used to do bareknuckle fighting, and on a drinking session with his mate he'd taken a bar fight for a bet. Fortunately, he'd won and they'd come back with a big bundle of fish and chips for them all. His head was very badly cut and his shirt soaked in blood. His mate had asked Fred to find a darning needle and cotton. Then he'd sat down and sewed his dad's head up as the kids all ate their fish and chips.

Life got much better after they'd settled down with their mother and stepdad. Fred was able to get a job at the local paper mill as his stepfather was a boss there. Fred worked hard and did very well, ending up a foreman.

All this had happened quite a few years before we met. I didn't know when I met him then that it would make him so possessive. I'd never been interested in any other men and hated Fred when he interrogated me. I like to go to the pictures and although it's only to the Electric Picture House around the corner, he'll only let me go to the early matinee. He then gives me less than ten minutes to get home and examines my shoes to ensure I've no mud on them if I'm just a couple of minutes late. As if one man isn't enough to cook, clean and look after our kids for. Then wait on hand-and-foot when he comes home from work. This is what we are told a good wife does, and I've done that. Now it's all going to change.

The front door opens then bangs shut. I listen to his boots hitting the lino on the lobby floor. I'm so angry that I'm blazing, not a bit scared of him this time. I wait with the telegram ordering him to report for duty in my hand. He stops in the lobby to hang his work coat up and take off his boots. Then he walks through the door.

I wave the rotten piece of paper at him, "Why? WHY?" I can feel tears streaming down my face. "You didn't need to volunteer, you're exempt!"

"What's going on?" He closes the lobby door and glances at the unset table. "Where's mi dinner, are you sick?"

I jump up waving the paper in the air. "Three days! Am I sick? Sick of you more like! What have you done, enlisting? Selfish sod, how are we going live?"

He takes the paper off me, "That was quick", then says softly, "was going to tell you". He tries to cuddle me.

"Ger' off, you know what you've done!" I pummel his chest, "Deserting us. If you don't care for me, you should care for your kids".

"You know I care, I do two jobs". He catches my fists and makes me sit down. "I *have* to go, how do you think I feel, with everyone looking at me? A fit man! My brothers have all gone. I want to serve my country, to be with them".

"You want to leave us!" I rant, "I'll never forgive you". I do not realise it then but I *will* forgive him. My life is going to change forever, I soon learn that too, of a freedom I haven't yet dreamed of.

He shrugs, "I've often told you I want to serve my country. I need to go".

I was naïve, that's what I was. What I didn't realise was how little he cares for us. He leaves a couple of days later.

After he leaves, I hardly hear from him. I find out he's spending his leave time with his brothers in Liverpool, Ireland, even France. He doesn't tell me what he's doing in his few and far between letters, saying he couldn't write much as they would be censored. Then I find out about the leaves he has had but not told me about, and only because his younger half-sister Hazel innocently let it slip about his not coming home on leave as she thought I knew. I feel totally and completely deserted. I see him once again, just before he embarks to his destination abroad. It's awkward. I don't tell him that I know about the times he didn't come home when he could have. I feel he is a stranger already.

* * * * *

Hell! I'd thought it was hard when Fred was here but his army wage is less than half the money he used to earn. So I start a couple of part-time jobs, which help. I've always wanted to work but never thought I would have to go back to doing housework for someone else. Now I work in the afternoons at a big house up Abbey Road. Oh the irony! In service all those years ago, Fred thought I was too good for it but he's forced me to have to do it again. I have to work very hard to pay the bills and look after the kids. Mother is good and looks after them when I have to work extra hours at the weekend.

My Abbey Road employers are an older couple and treat me very well, really appreciating what I do for them. It isn't like service was when I was a young girl, in fact they are always giving me little treats for the kids as well as myself. A few sweets here and there, a couple of apples, even eggs now and again. They have a local farmer friend who calls in, bringing eggs, butter and ham for them. I notice they pay him though so it must be black market. Still, when he leaves I am always offered a thick slice of delicious ham on a sandwich with butter on the bread. So I'm quite happy.

In the early mornings before I work at Abbey Road house, I drive a horse-and-milk cart for the Cooperative Dairy. It didn't take me long to learn how to do it either. My horse is a huge but gentle mare called Daisy. I enjoy taking her out and love meeting people.

Tom's started to run a bit wild but he's a good lad at heart, I know he won't get into trouble. Jane is the worry. "Mam this, Mam that", she drives me mad and is as demanding as ever. I just don't have the time to listen to her prattling on. Although I'm not there when she gets home from the Infants' School, I know she's safe. My jobs run together, one after the other, and I usually get home between 4.30-5.00pm so our backyard gate and scullery doors are always kept unlocked for her. There are always neighbours around and we all look after each other's kids, I do the same for them when I'm at home. Still, I've warned her that she must not go into a house with any stranger, especially a man.

Our Bella's always asking me to go to the dances with her. She says it will be good for me, give me something to smile about. She has no idea how difficult it is for us. She's single so is clearly having a wonderful time as the town is full of servicemen as well as other working men who've been called upon from other towns to work in our shipyard. Everywhere is packed out of a night and the pubs and dance halls are bouncing. Our Bella's having so much fun! I'm really jealous and very tempted. I love to dance so much. Fred never danced with me after our wedding night. It was as if he'd changed into a different person the minute we got married. All he did before he joined the army was work, then every night he'd have a pint with his workmates before coming home for his tea.

Even on Sundays in the summer, during the years before this damned war, Fred didn't join us on the beach much. There were lots of other family men though there, sporting knotted hankies to prevent their balding heads from burning, with their braces hanging down past their trousers! I loved it at the beach, we would spend the whole day just browsing in the sun. Everyone looked so healthy and the kids would get as brown as berries. For us mothers, it was bliss.

We would take our own teapots filled with tealeaves to the tiny kiosk at the top of the bank, where they would fill it with boiling water for the price of a penny, and it would start off being strong and tasty. A bit later in the day, we would have our teapots filled again – it would be a bit weaker but still good. Nearer teatime, when the kids came back from playing, having drank all their water and eaten their jam sandwiches, we would traipse up for a third fill up. We used to say it looked like 'piddle willy' but it warmed the kids up and they didn't care how it was so long as it had sugar in it!

Figure 4 – A Happy Family (not us!) Enjoying Tea on Biggar Bank

The kids would give us adults a peaceful day off doing their own thing, paddling and swimming. They used to build a den for themselves down where the large pebbles were and we didn't see them again until it was around 5pm clock, only coming back to eat and drink when they were usually snot-nosed, covered in sand and freezing! We cleaned and warmed them up with a brisk rub down. They were so hungry they wolfed down everything we gave them to eat and then we would set off to walk the two or three miles home.

When we finally arrived back home, it was a quick wash and straight to bed. The kids were always worn out with so much sun and fresh air that they didn't argue about bed! Total bliss for me! I would sit down and relax with my ciggie and a cuppa. I didn't even have to make Fred his tea if he hadn't come with us as I always left him with a ham salad for his dinner, and cheese sandwiches for tea. Although he wasn't too keen on me not being there to wait on him, he'd learnt not to moan after he realised he was lucky to have a day to himself. He always had a pint or two in the pub with his mates followed by a snooze when he came home. I used to make our Sunday roast on the Monday so that he didn't miss out.

But now we can't go any more. All local beaches are off limits because the Authorities fear the German's planes might land on the sands when the tide is out, or a German 'U' boat might send men in to infiltrate us. So our beaches have been mined, with rolls and rolls of barbed wire installed to keep us out. The mines have already killed two boys; you know what lads are like, always thinking it won't happen to them. Trees have also been felled, their trunks painted black and placed along the grass banks pointing towards the sky. The shipyard hasn't enough big guns yet and they hope the enemy will think they are real guns. Just another nice thing those damned Germans have deprived us of.

I have decided I do need cheering up and would like to go out dancing - if it wasn't for the kids. After all, Fred has done what *he* wants to do without thinking about me. But I can't leave the kids on their own and Mother won't mind them of a night. She says she does enough having them during the day and when I work weekends. So I've worked out a plan. But I can't leave them at the moment anyway as the town has started to have much more serious air raids. Dad's fixed our kitchen table up to protect us by hammering some thick tin under the top, and we have to sit underneath when there's a raid. He's installed it against the stair wall, as stairs are often the only thing left standing when a house receives a direct hit by a bomb. I don't think the table will be much good or save us if we do have a direct hit though. I think we should have had a shelter built in the backyard by now but we seem to be at the back of the queue.

Figure 5 - Typical Backyard Air Raid Shelter (not ours!)

One of my friends on Walney Island (where our now off-limit beaches are) received a hit that was so close all the windows blew out and a bedroom was totally wrecked. Luckily, not one member of the family was hurt. Even with all that disaster and mess, she was laughing telling me about it, mainly because of what her young son was so upset about. His goldfishes had survived, swimming around in their bowl albeit beneath a thick layer of soot, his budgie was dead in its cage, but the thing that had really upset him was the fact that he had saved up all his pennies for a long time to buy a toy he'd really wanted - and they'd all fused together!

Even though things are a bit better moneywise with my working, I've had to take in a Mr Brown as our lodger; he has the parlour. It doesn't bother me as I wasn't using it anyway. I didn't have enough money to buy coal to light the fire in there. I did have to have the chimney swept which delighted the kids in the street. They thought it was quite exciting watching the brush popping out of the chimney pot.

They say that all the men who have come to work in the shipyard are earning double to what the men in the services are getting. Some of them are earning more than three pounds ten shillings a week, and that's without all the overtime! Mr Brown gives me five shillings for rent and gas, and a shilling extra for the couple of buckets of coal he has each week. He is very frugal, with the most miserable fire I've ever seen. He seems to manage to keep it going with about 2-3 pieces of coal in the bottom of the grate. What he does with all the money he earns I don't know. He never gets a letter from anyone and never leaves to go home to where he has come from. We don't really have a conversation as I haven't taken to him.

I think Fred should be here now, earning that extra money for us. Even when I try to be very careful, I have to spend a pound weekly just on basic food items. The rent's four and six a week, then the coal and gas is another four shillings. An extra loaf of bread and pint of milk is fourpence ha'penny. Clothes cost around five shillings a week, and our Tom wears his shoes and trousers out at an alarming rate.

I have to earn at least 15 shillings more than Fred's army money to survive. I get a lot less money from the army than I did when he was working at the paper mill. His army pay is awful. The most annoying thing is, I've always managed my housekeeping without getting into debt and I've found out now that if I had owed money and therefore been in debt, I would have been allowed extra money from the army. Life isn't fair. That's why I can't be civil to Mr Brown. I know it's not logical for me to blame him for how we are having to live but I do. When he first arrived, he used to come into my kitchen to cook his tea and got in my way. I've made it plain to him I cook first and that he comes in after me. So now he sneaks around, waiting for me to finish. Sometimes I feel guilty. Luckily he is often on nights at the shipyard and then in bed all day. Although I'm not sure he gets a lot of sleep especially when the kids are all playing out in the street.

Jane seems to like him though and he's quite kind to her, giving her a couple of sweets every week. Everyone spoils her. It's not fair either, Mr Brown never treats Tom and Jane doesn't let on when she has the sweets. I know it's because of me. How would I know he'd notice a few matches missing out of his drawers. Why does anyone want a whole drawer full of different matchboxes? I have a key to his room so I'm entitled to have a little look around now and again since he's settled in. He doesn't have a lot of possessions but oddly, he has this drawer full of matchboxes. I had run out of matches one day so told Tom to sneak a few out of a box but to remember to take them from one of the boxes underneath. Mr Brown knew; I don't know how? He asked Tom if he had taken them and he said yes. Our Tom is so honest. So I think that's why he doesn't get any sweets and why I still pinch a few matches if I need them. I don't like him and he doesn't like me. Still, he has to stay and I have to put up with him until this damned war is over.

CHAPTER THREE:
EXHAUSTED

I think to myself, *has it only been just over a week since Jane's fifth birthday?* It must be the worst week for everyone in the town's life! I can't believe we have survived these last few days. I live every minute now with a sense of dread. Will it be us next? We are all exhausted with the nightly bombings.

I remember the strangest thing. Many months ago, Lord Haw Haw came onto the wireless and told us that our town had not been forgotten. He was right! It didn't seem real when we heard it, more like a dream. But this is *not* a dream, it's a living nightmare coming true.

On 22nd May 1936, the German airship 'Hindenburg' flew over our town. It was so low it looked as if it might touch the rooftops. They said it was the largest flying object ever constructed. It returned 30th June the same year, once again flying over the town. Our Evening Mail reported its second visit with these words:

"No-one will object to this big monster of the air paying us periodical visits. So long as her mission is friendly and peaceful. But the Hindenburg has also destructive potentialities, and one can imagine the havoc and important damage she could inflict in a busy, industrial town such as ours. What if she was to visit us in times of war, with a load of bombs?"

People are saying it was a prophetic call from the Editor not to trust the Germans. In 1936, the Nazi regime was in full flow. There is a lot of talk about the fact that, at that time, they were seen to be taking photographs of our shipyard from the Hindenburg.

Figure 6 – The 'Hindenburg' Flies Over Walney, May 1936

These past few weeks, we have had such a hammering from the German Luftwaffe. I think we're very lucky to still be alive. The shipyard has had many bombs landing right on it but fortunately most missed the main points and some didn't even explode. Although sad, it's also incredibly lucky that only two men were killed in the last terrible raid. They were on the big shipyard crane at the time, and they say in the paper that they were blown off, dying instantly. The crane now looks like a broken skeleton. We can see it from the end of our street. My Tom is completely right when he says it looks like a wounded animal with its head hanging down. Because some of the bombs that landed on the shipyard didn't explode, everyone is saying it's a miracle.

During all this time, when the Blitz was at its worst, the brave workers at the shipyard have soldiered on, working day and night. It has never closed, running 24 hours per day seven days a week, the workers never letting the Blitz stop them. Much of the workforce is made up of women doing men's work including assembling weapons and even welding! They work every bit as hard as the men, turning up for all the hours they are asked.

Figure 7 – Barrow Shipyard Steel Foundry

All around our house, there are streets half down, looking like huge broken sores pouring water, bricks, plaster and soot across the roads. There are firemen everywhere trying to extinguish fires but as quickly as they damp down one, another flares up. Both the official air raid wardens and men from the streets are digging and scrabbling in the rubble. All have dirty and tired faces, eyes red from smoke and lack of sleep. I realise with an awful shock that many friends and old neighbours are gone forever. I meet other friends as we queue at the shops in town. They tell me about how near to death they have been.

Figure 8 - Aftermath of the Air Raids

As I pass the paper shop on the way home from work one teatime, I see *The Evening News* board has a report on it. It states that a large number of residents from Hill View Grove have had the luckiest escape of their lives. A high explosive bomb landed and blew up right in the middle of an allotment area in between the gardens of the houses. I just know it's our allotment, it's the only one up there. I still can't really believe it even as I read, then a neighbour sends her lad to let me know it's true as he's seen it on the way home from work. I rush home to get the kids but as usual Tom's nowhere in sight.

I take Jane with me to see if it's true as I don't want to believe it. But it is true, our allotment has completely gone, my only place of peace. I think it must be the worst thing that has happened to me and feel guilty at feeling so devastated; I'm not injured and none of my family are hurt, I haven't lost my life or any of my family. Many people I know have lost loved ones. Right now however, I am distraught.

The lovely elderly couple from the house next to our allotment have lost their entire home. They've had a narrow escape. It seems that dreadful night, they were in their shelter at the end of the garden and when the bomb exploded, the shelter slipped down into the crater in our allotment. The shelter had to be to be dragged out of the crater with the couple still in it. Luckily, they were both still alive with only minor injuries. I later found out they are now staying with a niece and her family in a small terraced house. It was easy for me to call on them as I delivered milk to them when I was out on my round. The niece was a nice woman and invited me in to see them.

It was such a small house! Only two up two down, very cramped compared to their own three bedroomed semi. However, although they were badly shaken up they didn't complain about it once to me. They constantly thanked God that they were still together and not badly hurt. They were sorry I'd lost the allotment and worried about not seeing Jane again. So many people are fond of her and love her prattling on, but they don't have to listen to her every day! I have promised them I will take her to visit sometime. I feel sad for them, they have had to leave the house they have lived in and loved for over 50 years because the damage is so bad. I don't know how they can be so brave.

As I stand on the edge of the crater looking into the gaping hole, I have to fight hysterics - yet all I've lost is my allotment. Unlike the neighbours on the other side of the allotment, who'd had their shelter split right along its length and were left looking up at the sky. They even had to dig their youngest daughter out from under a pile of earth, her blanket saving her from suffocating. These shelters are dug into the ground with their roofs covered in soil or turf laid onto corrugated sheets. At the end of their long garden had been a really large area of spare ground, with a huge amount of wood stacked there. Incendiary bombs had hit it and set the wood alight causing a terrific blaze. So my friends had to stay in their split and damaged shelter waiting for the 'all clear' to sound before they could leave it

Whilst they were crouching together in the small space, they'd heard the drone of a German bomber coming in very low. Terrified, they watched in horror as it fired its machine guns at the people who were trying to put out the raging fire, thank God they never killed anyone. As the mother told me about it, her eyes filled with tears. She said her 11-year-old daughter Lillian was very upset to think that even a German could shoot at those defenseless people.

I should be glad Dad did steal Fred's bicycle after all, it's better than the Gerries blowing it up along with everything else on the allotment. At least it helped pay one of his gambling debts. I don't know how Mother has put up with him over the years, he's taken everything that was precious to her. I've warned him that taking Fred's bike was the last straw and next time if the men he owed money to didn't kill him, I would.

I'm going to miss gardening at the allotment so much. When I worked up there digging and planting, I forgot everything. Even Jane lets me have a bit of peace. She insists the butterflies and bees talk to her so it's quiet and happy while we are there. She sits for hours under a tree, talking and singing to herself, or the old dears in their garden next door would call her over and she would keep them entertained for hours. They really spoilt her, I think she's going to miss them a lot. They never seemed to mind her prattling on. Now all that peace has gone. We both stand at the edge of the crater and cry.

Then I start to laugh, yet I know I haven't seen anything to laugh at. Jane looks at me, I can see she doesn't know why I'm laughing and I can't tell her because I don't know either. Everything is gone, blown away forever. We won't even have the few fresh eggs that the last three or four hens were laying for us. Where they are now God only knows. I guess they didn't get a chance to fly away.

We set off walking slowly home. I think it will be good for us both just to walk for a while, it might clear my head. Jane doesn't do her usual moaning saying her legs are tired.

Mrs Carr has called in, she'd heard me close the front door and knows I'll be ready for a brew. I often wished I could be like her, she's so laid back and takes everything in her stride. The kettle boils and I pour the water into the teapot, let it mash for a minute then pour the tea. I try to tell her what has happened but can't without filling up. She stands and cuddles me to her large bosom as I control myself a bit. We sit drinking tea and talk about our experiences from the night before. I've had to use my old metal teapot as my best one smashed during one of the last terrible nights we've had. As I show her all my broken, precious china and my shattered cabinet, I try not to cry again because she has so much less than me and never complains.

I feel sad as I pick up one of my china cups. "Look Mrs Carr, my china tea-set. Mother and Dad's wedding present to us, it was her mother's".

"Better that than one of the kids 'Lizbeth". She looks at me, shakes her head and pats my hand. Sometimes I hate her logic.

"I know you're right but I don't want to hear it off you, not right now", I sniff, feeling right sorry for myself. Everything normal in my life is disappearing, day by day, and I feel despair and anger. If Fred hadn't enlisted, things would have been a lot better. Mrs Carr's chest starts to shake with laughter and I think she's laughing at me. Then she tells me a tale that makes me feel ashamed.

"Aye lass, you're still here aren't you? I've just had a visit from my friend Aggie. Her daughter Amy had a bairn a couple of weeks ago. Her husband was called up just as she got pregnant and she hasn't seen him since so she's having to manage on her own. Aggie could only stay with her for a few days after the bairn was born. She's still got another five kids at home herself. Amy's one of them that had the high explosive bomb drop up at Hill View where your allotment was. She hasn't had a proper night in bed since the boy was born. When't siren goes, she's had to pick the bairn up in his sheets and blankets, put it under one arm, then carry his food and essentials in the other one. One of the nights when she climbed into their shelter, she went to put the baby down and found he had slipped out of the blankets. Luckily he'd dropped onto't lawn and when she found him he was still asleep and none't worse for the mishap. So I don't want to hear you complaining again".

I'm shocked, "That's dreadful, is she OK? Why are you laughing about it?"

She shakes her head and gives me one of her looks. "Luckily she was staying with her mam this week. She might not have been here after this lot". She was quite serious for once. "Lass, what else can you do but laugh? He was OK, didn't break anything or fall on his head. It must have looked funny. Even Aggie laughed when she was telling me about it. You have to try to get your sense of humour back 'Lizbeth".

She told me the Trevelyan Hotel in town had been completely destroyed. Her priest had visited and told her he had to go to the site to give the last rites to the people who had perished.

Figure 9 - Trevelyan Hotel Prior to the Bombing

I sniffed and said, "I'm sorry, I just feel so alone at times. If it wasn't for you I don't what I'd do". Mrs Carr gives me another big hug as she leaves, and I do feel a bit better.

* * * * *

At last! I had thought we were going to die under our table but now thank God, the builders have finally arrived in our backstreet. They are working fast and we will have a shelter in the backyard by tomorrow night. It is a barren looking thing. How we're going to sleep in it, I don't know, that's *if* we get any sleep. This past few nights the Luftwaffe have kept us all awake.

Our Tom can't go to school as there's been a lot of damage done to it. I'm told ceilings are down, windows are blown out and several doors are off their hinges. Of course, he loves this and wants to go out with his mates all the time. Today though, he is going to help me get our shelter ready whether he wants to or not. If these raids keep up, I think we'll have to spend a lot of time in it.

I've time to sort out what I can put into our shelter today because I can't go to work. It's impossible to take the milk out, there's been too much damage done to this part of the town this past couple of days.

A young lad from the dairy was sent to tell me it wouldn't be safe taking out the horse-and-milk cart as there are a number of large craters in many of our streets. I ask how my horse Daisy is. He says the horses were very frightened last night but seem OK today. They work so hard because the milk's delivered seven days a week, and I think a rest will be good for them. I just hope we have at least one quiet night! Daisy is so sweet. The milk lad's told me that the men and milk boys are delivering as much as they can using the old fashioned handcarts; I bet they never thought they would be used again.

So I have time to sort out any bedding and covers I can spare for the shelter. At least it's warmer this month. I need to put cushions and covers onto the wooden benches they've fixed around the shelter for us to sit or sleep on. I want to make them as comfortable as possible. I'm going to make a large rag rug to put on the floor. That'll keep Jane busy and out of my hair for hours, she loves sorting the colours into bundles.

Nothing will ever be the same again but we have to make the best of it. I've seen things I'll never ever forget. I feel as if I'll never be able to forgive Fred for deserting us like he has. All his family and friends tell me he did the right thing if only for his pride and for his country. But what about me? I need him.

CHAPTER FOUR:
EVACUATION

I'm not sure we're that much safer in the shelter, there have been quite a lot of people killed in them. But because our street is on a hill, the shelters at the bottom get flooded when it rains which means the occupants have to sit with their Wellingtons on, so I shouldn't complain as it's very cold and uncomfortable for them. I've done the best I can with ours. What, with the smells and having to share it with Mr Brown when he isn't on nights, it isn't easy. Jane moans all the time about the paraffin lamp, Tom complains about having to wee in the bucket but I've sorted that out.

Coming out of the shelter when the 'all clear' goes, I always get upset because the sky is lit with a red glow from the streets that are still burning. Sometimes there are loud explosions with sparks and massive flames shooting up into the sky.

Our Tom is crazy about collecting shrapnel, I have to watch he doesn't leave the shelter before the 'all clear' sounds. He comes home with all kinds of things he says he swaps it for. I don't mind marbles or the odd ha'penny, but I found a penknife in his pocket which he insists he swapped a piece of shrapnel for. He worries me some times! He has made a friend of Rick, a lad two or three years older than him from a few streets away. I can see he's very impressed with this Rick and he's moved away from his street gang to knock around with him. I've been warned by some of the neighbours that Rick is a pretty crooked lad and a good candidate for Borstal if he isn't careful. His mother is so fat it has disabled her and she can't leave the house. There are six or seven other kids who just seem to be allowed to run wild. I'm sure most of the time she doesn't know what any of them are doing. Still, when I talk to Tom about it, he promises me they don't do anything wrong.

It's been a bit quieter this past week or two so we've had a few nights in our beds. Jane decided she had a sore throat but I didn't believe her at first. I know she fakes it when she tries to get an extra day off school. Now though, she kept me up most of one night and I realise she is feeling bad. I have to have a couple of hours off the next day to take her to the Doctor, who takes one look, says it's her tonsils and sends us to the hospital to see the Ear, Nose and Throat Specialist. The outcome is she goes unwillingly into hospital three days later and stays nearly a week after having them removed. I have peace for nearly a week! It hurts her to talk and I can't take time off from work so Mother has her at her house. I'm sorry for her but not having to listen to her incessant chatter is nice. I don't know why girls are so different to boys; our Tom comes in, eats, and leaves as soon as I let him.

Today I receive quite a shock when they bring letters home from school. Even though there have been rumours, and some kids have already left, it's still a shock. Now I have to make the decision whether to let them go away. I wouldn't mind letting Jane go, she ties me down so much more than Tom. Being a girl, I have to keep an eye on her to make sure she's safe. Evacuation, it's a lot to think about.

One day, very recently, Jane and me had gone to the pictures. I often think about how easy we could have been killed that day and still shake when I think how we could have been shot to death. It's hard to believe it could really happen and in broad daylight.

The town is a bit wild now and full of strangers. We all hear stories of women being frightened by strange men. Our Nellie (who is an insurance woman so has to go out collecting money on a Friday night because most people get paid then) has had a terrible scare. She is tiny, quite timid and well-mannered but was attacked on her way home from collecting insurance a couple of weeks ago. Two soldiers tried to drag her along with them. They were drunk, aggressive and frightened her to death. Although only 6pm, it was very dark, making it unsafe for everyone, due to both heavy fog as well as the gas lamps in the streets remaining unlit because of the air raids. So our Nellie only had her torch which was mostly covered in tape with only a slit of light left to show her where to put her feet.

Thankfully, she'd had the common sense to put her handbag through a nearby house window and of course the soldiers immediately ran off. The police said she did the right thing, though I don't think the householder was too pleased as it's not easy to get glass replaced. The police have warned all women not to walk on their own of a night when it's dark and always to carry a whistle if they must go out.

I decide I should go next door to ask Mrs Carr what she thinks about the kids being evacuated. I'm sure she will have received the same letter, although her kids go to the Catholic school, Saint Teresa's. I always knock on her door hard. I know they won't hear me otherwise as they are such a big, boisterous family. So after knocking, I open the door and walk up the lobby. When I open the door to go into the kitchen, I have to shout over the noise.

"Hiya Mrs Carr, I wanted to ask what are you doing about the kids being evacuated." She has five kids and the oldest boy is only ten, but they don't worry her as much as my two do me.

"Evacuation! Not me, who would ever cope with my five?" She cleans a heap of ironing off a chair, "Sit down lass, I'll pour you a cuppa".

"It's OK", I sit down and signal with my hand I don't want one, "Just had one thanks". I think the world of Mrs Carr, she's my best friend but I can't drink her tea, she leaves the teapot stewing on top of the range all day. Every so often, she will put a teaspoon of fresh tealeaves on top of what's in the pot already. By the end of the day it's like drinking tar.

"Are you sure you aren't going to send your kids to be evacuated? It's so dangerous now with all the bombing".

"No, I'm not; I'd have to go with them and then who'd look after t'old man?"

"Well, I'm thinking of letting my two go. Letter says they'll be well looked after and I'm finding it very hard both looking after them and working full-time. You know how demanding Jane is".

"She just wants your attention. She's only just five you know?"

"I know but she never stops, 'Mam, Mam, Mam', all the time. All your five together aren't like it".

"Come on 'Lizbeth, my five have each other and your Tom's a real lad, he's no time for girls *especially* little sisters".

"I know, that's why I'm going to let her go".

"You can't send one without t'other, surely".

I can tell she's shocked, "No 'course not, I mean both of them".

"You know lass, she's a nice little girl, they can't all be boys you know".

"Mrs Carr, I take good care of her". I am annoyed with her and protest. "I keep her nice, everyone tells me how nice her hair is and she's always dressed well and very clean".

"I know love, but that's you. I could eat my food off your kitchen flags. You expect too much of yourself and Jane. Remember, she's still a baby and we all are suffering".

"That's why I am going to let her go, she needs to be safe and I need some time to myself". I leave to make our tea and reread the letter. I decide to go to school tomorrow to listen to what the Headmistress has to say. She'll tell us about when they have to go and where they will go.

Tom has just come in to eat and hands me a packet of tea. I take it and ask, "Where did you get this?"

"Found it". He looks guilty.

I grab his ear and pull him to me, "Found it?"

He tries to pull away. "Ger' off Mam, you're hurting".

He starts to cry so I leave go. "No-one loses *tea*, did you get it of that mate of yours?"

"No, I did a message for an old lady, she giv' it me".

"Then why did you tell me you found it?" I grab his arm and look right into his face. "Now tell me the truth".

"She did giv' it me, honest Mam. I thought you'd be mad at me taking it off an old lady just for doing a message".

I'm not sure what the truth is. He is usually a good lad though so I give him the benefit of the doubt. Still, he's made my mind up; he's going as well. At least I know he will be safe and away from temptation. Now it is settled and I have decided to let them both go, I feel quite happy about it. I think to myself *it's better than being blown apart like many of my friends, neighbours and families have been.*

* * * * *

Today is the day they are leaving. Last night I made them a special tea: bacon, egg and fried bread. I've also cooked them a proper rice pudding, plenty of milk and sugar and finished the top off with the last of the nutmeg. It has made a lovely brown skin on the top and they love it. They call it *Grandad's Toffee* because Dad gives them a bit each off the top of his rice pudding whenever they're over there.

Then I gave them a bath and made sure their heads were clean. I bet the people who take them will really check them over. Of course, I wouldn't blame them because there are some rough kids going. I hope, because they look so clean, they will be chosen by a nice family. Although I'm sure I shouldn't worry because the families that take them in will have to take good care of them. I packed their boxes last night because I have to work and can't stay to see them off so am going to drop them off at Mother's house. Usually I let Tom take Jane but for once I'm going to be late for work. Mother will see them off and I've made sure they have everything they need. Saying goodbye is hard, even my Tom looks as if he is going to cry.

I say, "Come on, you're the man of the house, you have to be brave and look after Jane".

He hugs me and I kiss him which really embarrasses him. He wipes his mouth, "Ugh Mam, what did you do that for?" I think to myself *at least that stopped the tears.* All this time, Jane is standing beside us sobbing.

I hug her and pat her on the head. "Now then, stop crying and be a big girl, you're going to have a nice run out to the countryside and probably a picnic". That cheered her up a bit. I had to leave before I showed I was upset or we would have more tears. I was just finding it so hard looking after them and working as well.

At first it felt very strange, walking into the empty house at the end of the day. Surprisingly I soon become used to it.

CHAPTER FIVE:
CHANGES

Surprisingly, being on my own has made my life a lot easier. I can come and go as I please and I'm not tired like I was when the kids were here. I do a lot more now, and have started to go out with Bella when I'm home. Dad isn't happy about it but I think he believes me when I tell him I don't do anything I shouldn't. I never hear much from Fred, apparently he isn't allowed to write often. It seems to me we have lost him already and I find I don't miss him like I thought I would. Now my freedom is so precious, I know when he comes back nothing is going to be the same.

I am so busy I don't know how I managed with two kids at home. Since I've been going out with our Bella, I've been on a diet. I thought it would be hard but the weight has dropped off and I feel wonderful. I would just nibble dry cream crackers and drink weak tea all day instead of eating meals. One of Bella's friends told me she has lost two stone by doing this diet. It has worked quickly for me because I didn't need to lose so much.

Bella and me go dancing every weekend when we can. I've learnt to jive and you need to be slim for that. It has made me feel so alive and happy again. I had learnt to do the Charleston before I met Fred and loved it. Although he didn't like me doing that kind of dancing, said it made me look like I was a fast sort of girl. So I never did it when he was around. Still, when I did the housework and he wasn't there, I used to Charleston around the room to the music on the wireless. I think that's why I've found it so easy to jive.

Now I feel like the young girl I was all those years ago. I've grown my hair longer and put henna on it so it's a lovely shade of mahogany. I make a roll of it across the top of my head with an old silk stocking, which is really fashionable these days. I have bought myself two new snoods, one pink and the other green. They hold the long hair at the back in a roll and I feel so glamorous. People tell me I look like one of the film stars. I dance the whole night when we go out because I get asked up so often. I'm getting a lot of admirers at the dances and I'm asked for dates from a lot of the men there. But I never go out, or home, with anyone (though I do get very tempted!).

Bella and me went on the train to Blackpool for a day out. I know there's a war on but I think we deserved the day away. We went to an afternoon show and it cost us threepence. The advert says its *"Epstein's Latest Sensation!"* and was called *"Jacob & the Angel"*. It was for adults only and we were quite shocked, it was so exciting. Still, we won't tell Mother and Dad.

When we came out, we bought a jug of tea to have on the beach. I had also brought sandwiches for us so we sat and ate them, then treated ourselves to a huge, penny ice-cream cornet. They were good and we enjoyed them immensely as we walked along the Promenade. We had such a good laugh as we wandered along. There were quite a few men who whistled and tried to talk to us but we were enjoying it being just the two of us without a worrying thought in our heads. So we enjoyed the moment and passed by, being happy in each other's company.

We had to get the train back home at teatime as we were both working the next day. The train was packed on the way home. We were lucky to get into a carriage with the last two seats together. The other six people in the carriage were all older people and very friendly. We were both very tired and sat quietly for a short time. I sat back with my eyes closed, enjoying the *clickity clack* of the train wheels and the hissing of the steam as we rushed along. Then a nice older lady who was sitting next to me started to talk to us.

"Where are you two young ladies getting off at?" She asked.

I was startled; my mind had been miles away. "We are going to Barrow", I replied.

She smiled, "I only asked because you both seem tired and I didn't want you to miss your stop if you dozed off".

In the next breath, she offered us a packet with some tiny sandwiches in. "Would you like a sandwich?" She asked. I'm really hungry as well as tired, so gratefully took one and so did Bella.

"Thank you very much", we both said at once. It was small and dainty, and didn't fill up much of the hole in my stomach but I was really grateful. Then she offered the packet around the carriage. A couple of men took one, others said *thank you* but they'd brought their own. It must have made them all hungry as everyone started bringing out packets of food from bags and baskets. I realised we should have brought some sandwiches for later. Then, as they ate, everyone started talking to each other and we were offered another sandwich and a couple of homemade biscuits.

An older man who was with his wife said, "I heard you say where you were from". He paused, "Aye you've had it bad over there, well that's what I've heard, is it right?"

I hesitate, he looks an old retired country type of gentleman and harmless. But we are always told the walls have ears and to beware of loose tongues. I know they don't put everything that has happened to our shipyard town in the newspapers. There are always rumours going about that there are spies in our town and people swear they have seen lights being flashed out to sea from the slag banks.

The old man realises I'm being very wary and says seriously, "You know lass, I'm as much a Lancashire lad as you are a Lancashire lass".

His wife puts her hand on his arm, "Now then love, she's right to hesitate. We aren't offended dear, you're doing the right thing, we understand".

Her husband says, "She's right duck, I never thought".

"And I'm sorry", I say, "I didn't mean to be rude to any of you". I nod around everyone who is sitting there.

The old man smiles and pats my knee. "This was the train I used to drive for many years. I retired four years ago in 1938 just before the war was declared. We often turned around in Barrow. I've fond memories of those passengers. In fact if I hadn't been losing my eyesight, I would be called back; I could have been driving this one".

His wife spoke up, "You know how much pay they get now? We would be very well off, three pounds ten shillings a week. Even a labourer gets two pounds two shillings and sixpence, and some even get two pounds ten shillings. The most we used to get was two pounds two shillings and sixpence and he was paid extra because he was a train driver. Then he would get another five shillings with overtime if he was lucky. I don't know how others managed on less. My budget was one pound for food, 10 bob rent, 4 bob for heating and light, and clothing took about eight bob. His overtime paid for our holidays".

I sit quiet, knowing how angry I am about my paltry one pound eight shillings a week that the army pays me for taking my husband away. It's costing me fivepence for a stone of potatoes - that's when I can buy a stone. It's usually only half of a stone for each person when we queue up now. And they charge threepence, which makes more profit for the shopkeeper. It's as if some of the people in Britain who aren't in the forces are making money out of the war in every way they can.

Everyone had been quiet while the old lady was angrily getting it off her chest, it was what most of us felt. When she finished, she apologised. "Sorry, I get so mad".

Her husband, held her hand, "Lottie love, don't go on, we are lucky, think of the people who earn much less than that a week".

There was general agreement that she was right to moan. Then everyone just started to talk about the nice day out they'd all had in Blackpool. By that time, we were stopping at stations and the old couple left at Grange, still apologising. She shoved the rest of their picnic bag into my hands as she left.

"Here love, this should keep you going until you get home". I only had time to say thanks before they were gone and the whistle went to say we were pulling out of the station. When I opened the bags there were three fresh scones, two sausage rolls and some more biscuits. There were only two other passengers left in our carriage and they had eaten. Selfishly, I decided to share the food between me and Bella. I had to wake her up to eat as she had slept almost all the way home.

She ate everything I handed to her then asked, "Where did you get this?"

I just laughed and said, "Don't ask". I thought to myself it was a lovely meal at the end of a really great day.

* * * * *

I hardly ever see Mr Brown although he still lives here. It suits me and I'm sure he feels the same. I feel a bit sorry for him if there is a raid on when he isn't on nights. He's scared when he has to go down to the shelter even if I'm there but now he's often on his own. Still, he leaves his five shillings on my kitchen table every Friday night and that's fine.

It's funny but the raids have been less often since the kids were evacuated. I did feel awful at first letting them go but I know they are safer where they are. I go home with Bella, staying with Mother and Dad if there is a warning and we have to leave the dance hall early. Bella and me share her single bed then. I giggle about the men we have danced with as if I'm the girl I was ten years ago. Bella has so many young men asking her out, it's hard for her deciding whom to go out with.

I cannot believe it when Grace's mam (mother of the little girl who was evacuated alongside Jane and Tom) comes to see me; she is so upset. I ask her in and pull out a chair for her to sit on. Then put the kettle on the hook over the fire. It sits on the oven top all day which keeps it hot, so starts to sing right away.

As she sits down she says, "It's Grace. I'm going to bring her home right away", she just about stops herself from crying.

I pass her a cup of tea and ask her, "What's happened?"

She sits drinking her tea, saying nothing, and I wait until she can pull herself together. Then she starts to tell me and I'm so shocked.

"Grace's teacher phoned the school and told the Headmistress, Miss Brown, what has happened. She came to see me and explained what the teacher had told her. It seems my Grace has been touched".

I'm still not sure, "Touched?"

"Yes by a farm lad".

I interrupt her, "What about Jane?"

"No Jane is OK but Miss Brown thinks you should come with me to see her".

I interrupt, "I'm surprised she didn't come to see me. I'm annoyed and think she should have been in touch with me as well". I am angry and even though she says Jane is OK, I think I should have been told.

Grace's mam shakes her head, "You know how busy she is. I offered to come round to see you. I can tell you all you want to know, or at least as much as she could tell me".

We sit looking at each other and I know how she must feel. I think to myself, *I'm glad Jane is OK*. Not being sure what to say I wait; she is so upset.

Then she says, "I'm sorry, I don't even know your name, Grace always calls you "Jane's mam". I realise this is only the second time we've spoken and that was only to say hello when we met at school months ago".

I touch her hand, "Of course, and I should have asked you your name. I'm Elizabeth".

"My name's May", she stands up and holds her hand out.

"Oh sit down love," I take her hand and hold it. "Now tell me what arrangements have been made?"

"I'm getting the 10am train tomorrow. It takes me to Kendal then there's a bus to the village".

I have to think and say, "I can't get off work just like that, I'll have to let them know at work. Can't we go the day after? I don't like letting work down".

May looks at me as if I'm the wicked stepmother, "No I'm not leaving Grace there another day", she says, "I'll go on my own".

"No no, of course you won't. I'll let work know tonight". I stand up, "In fact I'll walk part of the way with you now. You live near the phone box don't you?" I walk to the lobby and put my coat on.

May stands up and says, "How should we meet?"

"I'll knock you about 9.30? It's only ten minutes to the station from your house".

As we walk along together. I can see how shocked and worried she is. I think to myself, *what if it had been Jane?* I realise that although I have problems with Jane, I would be as mad as hell if it was her. I left May at her front door and reassured her again that I would be there at 9.30. The boss isn't happy about such short notice until I explain the situation then he's so angry he even says I won't lose my day's pay.

I haven't been back at home for more than five minutes when there's a knock at the door and Mrs Carr walks in.

"Have we time for a cuppa 'Lizbeth? Those kids next door are driving me up the wall".

I laugh, "Your kids?"

"Do you think I'd have a houseful like them if they weren't mine?" Her huge bosom heaves with laughter.

I shake my head at her, "I don't know how you manage, Mrs Carr".

"OK," she says, "I might have a few kids but I don't miss much. What was May doing calling on you today? I didn't know you were friends with her".

I tell her the story, "I'm going with her tomorrow although Jane's alright. Miss Brown thinks I should go as well because they are billeted together. Do you think I need to go? I have to have tomorrow off and I'm letting work down".

She looks at me, shocked. "I don't know why you've even

thought about it, 'Lizbeth sometimes you really shock me".

"Well she's alright and from what I can gather, the boy has been sent away".

Mrs Carr pours herself another cup of tea. "Just go", she says.

"I am going. I only asked you what you thought".

"You're doing the right thing lass and it's time you visited her. You need to find out what kind of people are taking care of your bairn".

"I think she'll be fine, they have a small girl of their own". I can't see there will be a problem but I realise I should go.

I get up very early the next morning so that I can make myself look smart. I bet Jane will be surprised when she sees me. I call at May's house as I promised, right on 9.30. She looks as if it's just any other day. I'm surprised she hasn't appeared to make much effort with herself. She asks me in and I realise why. She's three small children who all appear to want to cling to her skirt. Her sister is there to take care of May's kids who also has three small children with her. We are leaving quite a houseful. May picks up her coat and shakes the kids off. As we leave the house, she kisses them all, closes the kitchen door and walks up the lobby. I'm sure I can hear every one of the children howling as May closes the front door behind us.

She sets off and I look at her. "How on earth will your sister manage six of them?" I'm shocked at her calm exterior. "I can't manage two when they start".

She laughs, "The more you have the easier it gets. I'm sure as soon as I closed the door, they stopped wailing and found something else to do. You worry too much".

We walk along the street not talking to each other. I think about what I'm going to do if I have to take Jane away from the farm.

CHAPTER SIX:
MORE MOVES

When we arrive at Barrow Central railway station, I see how bad things really are after the last air raid attack. The whole station is an absolute mess. Thank God, in amongst all this chaos, the rail lines are still intact so the rail service is still working.

We sit quietly on the train and I think about the damage the Germans have caused and how lucky we are to be using the train today.

Figure 10 – Entrance to Barrow Rail Station Prior to the Blitz

What had happened was that on one of the recent night raids, the German planes followed the train lines, flying low and following right along the tracks, bombing each station as they came to them. Luckily, they mostly hit the nearby railway buildings and didn't do too much damage to the lines. The few that were affected were fixed very quickly. Still, they've made a terrible mess of our lovely Victorian station. It is in such an awful state. It will have to be rebuilt one day and I'm sure it will never be as beautiful.

Figure 11 - Barrow Rail Station, after the Blitz

We have a couple of smaller stations on the edge of the town. One of them is next to the ruins of our Furness Abbey. Thank goodness they didn't manage to drop any bombs on the abbey itself, which dates back to the 1100s. The small picturesque station stands beside the *Furness Abbey Hotel*, a huge manor house that was empty for a long time until bought by the Furness Railway in 1847 and opened as a hotel.

Figure 12 - Furness Abbey Hotel, Railway Station & the Abbey Ruins

(Old photograph of a picturesque valley near the edge of town, showing the ruins of our 12th century Furness Abbey (immediate foreground) partially obscured by trees (and still standing to this day), the huge sandstone house known as *Furness Abbey Hotel* at top left, with the nearby Furness Abbey railway station shown towards the top middle of the image, its tracks heading diagonally through the trees).

Now the hotel has been taken over by the army and is full to overflowing with soldiers. They were very lucky because although it was badly damaged in parts, it's still habitable. They are the 'Z' battery and keep jeeps and anti-aircraft guns in what used to be the stables-and-tack room.

Next to the stables is the garage where Bella's friend Gwen, her mother, dad, younger sister and brother all live. Many years before, it had been the Coach House where horse-and-coaches would stop. It's the *Furness Abbey Garage* now with one petrol pump. The locals call it 'FAG' for short. Gwen's dad looks after the garage and her mam helps at the Abbey Hotel just across the road. She helps to cook for the soldiers which is great because she gets quite a lot of unofficial goods to take home. Whenever she has visitors, they always get a plate with a couple of eggs and a slice or two of bacon on it.

The soldiers are a great gang of men, most of them are cheerful and you never hear them moaning about hard times. We meet a lot of them at the dances and have a good laugh with them.

The night of this particular bombing, both the garage and house were badly damaged. All the doors, windows and parts of the roof were blown off. Gwen's family have stayed because they can still use the range for cooking and luckily, as the petrol pump didn't blow up, her dad serves petrol. If it had done so they wouldn't be here to tell the tale!

Gwen's dad has cleaned out his unused and very large henhouse and they all sleep in there now. I think they have eaten all the hens as there are no pet hens kept here during wartime. They've laid their mattresses on the floor around the edge of the henhouse. That's including an extra one for the manager and his wife from the hotel as their flat was also wrecked in the bombing. Gwen laughed as she told us there were seven people, the dog and the cat in there.

There was a bucket placed in the middle of the floor should they want a wee in the night but one time, Gwen just *had* to go to the lav' after coming in from the dance. We all drank too much orange cordial because we got so hot with all that jiving. She was too shy and embarrassed to use the bucket so decided to go to the outside lav' before she going in the house. It was a really dark night and pouring with rain so she'd rushed in to the lav' in the dark and sat down quickly…onto someone's knee! She said, 'I don't know who screamed the loudest, me or the sentry who was guarding the guns that night and had sheltered in the lav!''. When she told us girls, we thought it was so funny. I thought to myself, *if she'd wanted to go so badly how did she hold it after that scare?* I didn't ask but I bet she was glad it was dark!

Figure 14 – The Furness Abbey Hotel

(Old photograph of the *Furness Abbey Hotel* used by the army during the war, as viewed from its tennis courts at the front of the house. The nearby railway station is located out of shot on its right).

We've arrived at our station and as we get off the train, I realise we haven't really talked since we first got on. May has been deep in her own thoughts. I can see how drawn her face is. I feel quite guilty, I haven't had to dwell on the things she has. Perhaps I should have talked to her to keep her mind off it but I'd so enjoyed sitting, thinking and listening to the rhythm of the train, it was almost hypnotic. When we get off, it's only around the corner to the bus station and we have timed it just right, the bus is waiting.

As we get on I say, "This is lucky, it's saved us an hour's wait although we would have had time for a cup of tea".

May just shrugs her shoulders, "I just want to get there".

I hug her, "Of course but cheer up, you don't want Grace to see you like this. She'll wonder what the matter is. I bet she's already forgotten about the--- well, you know what I mean".

When we near our destination, we get off the bus and walk down a lovely country road, arriving at a small hall as our instructions had said we would. I feel nervous as we walk into the hall. The pretty and very pleasant young woman who comes to greet us as we stand inside the door only looks about 18. It's quite a surprise when she holds her hand out and introduces herself. She is the teacher.

The children are all lying down on camp beds but none are asleep now we've come in. Jane starts to get up and calls out to me. Her teacher quietly tells her she must stay there until she tells them all to get up. She signals May and me over to the corner where her desk and some small chairs are. We both perch on the chairs and listen as she puts us in the picture. I know how bad May must feel, I'm boiling with temper. The lad has just been sent away and it's obvious they want to keep everything quiet. I think to myself, *he could always do it again.*

May sits, listening quietly then says, "I just want to take my Grace home and to forget all about it. She wasn't hurt and in time, she won't even think about it. We'll all forget. But she'll never leave us again until she's grown up. I'd rather we were blown up together than her be in danger without her family there". She stands up. "I'm sorry but I want to go now, I can't bear her being here any longer".

Her teacher says, "I'll get you her bundle". She looks as if she's going to cry as she stands up. She goes over to Grace, whispers to her and she starts to get off the bed. It was a message to all the other kids and they all start to get up, of course Jane is one of the first. She charges over to me and sits on my knee. I can see she thought she was coming home as well. May and Grace hug her when they realise we aren't leaving with them. I am glad they don't hang around as it is hard enough work explaining to Jane why we aren't leaving.

When I walk across the road with Jane at 3.30pm after school finishes, I think of all the things her teacher has told me. I don't think I'm going to like these people she's been staying with but I will listen to what they have to say. Jane pulls my hand as she leads me to the house. It has a very pretty doorway with seats either side. I knock the door but Jane sits on one of the seats and pats the place beside her.

She says, "No Mam, they aren't here yet, they work in the fields. We have to wait here for them".

I sit on the seat facing her, "Oh well it's a nice place to sit isn't it?"

"Yeh, and me and Grace play house in it. Not any more though cos me and you are going home, aren't we?"

It's easier not to answer so I just smile at her. Sit and think about what I should do if I don't think she can stay with them. We wait and wait, Jane needs a wee and so do I. When I ask her where the lav' is, it's quite a surprise. She jumps off the seat, "Come on Mam, we can wee together".

She takes me down a path behind the pretty farmhouse and there in front of us is a small hut. We have an outside lav' at home but this hut is much bigger. When Jane opens the door, she proudly shows me how we can sit together. I've never seen a two-seater lav' before, some of the houses at home still have the old fashioned wooden seat with one hole but not two! Jane really wants us to sit together so I do what she wants. It stinks and how one of the kids hasn't fallen through one of the rather large holes I'll never know. We go back to the doorway and sit there for a long time, by now I really need a cup of tea.

"Jane, where are they?" I ask. As if she would know where they were.

"It's OK," she says, "They always come back".

And they did, after 5.30pm. We have been sitting outside for two hours. I realise they had left Jane to wait on her own, knowing that Grace was leaving earlier. I am flaming mad and ready to have a go right away.

When they finally arrive back, the huge young man comes towards me smiling and holding out his hand to shake mine. He is around 6' tall, very muscular, has a hard look and the florid complexion of someone who works outside in all weather. I think to myself, *I wouldn't like to cross him!* He looks like the type who would always have his own way. He doesn't introduce himself or ask my name, just says, "Sorry, we're later than we meant to be, something held us up and you can't just drop everything when you're dealing with livestock. Come in, my wife will put the kettle on".

I feel he is challenging me right away so I wait to see what they have to say. His wife is also large and quite homely. Mrs Carr always has a nice turn of phrase for everything and probably would have said, "Poor woman, she must have been the last in the queue when God gave looks out". Strangely, their small girl who is about two years old is very pretty. I smile at he, but she's very shy and hangs onto her mam's skirt.

The woman nods at me and leads the way into the house. We go into a very large kitchen which, even though it's nice outside, is very cold. It's large, dark and sparsely furnished, not the comfortable homely kitchen I had expected. When the man comes in, he goes straight to the huge, open fireplace and throws some logs into the grate. They are stacked up in the alcoves that sit either side of the huge range. The low embers in the grate don't look bright enough to ignite the logs but they must have been very dry as they flare up into flames very quickly, making the kitchen appear much more cheerful.

"Sit down", he says, pulling a chair out for me. The woman puts the small girl into a high chair and gives her a crust to chew on. She smiles and whispers to her, making the child smile back. I think she must have some kindness in her and think perhaps Jane is exaggerating when she's told me the things she has had done to her. Then I remember it isn't just her that has told me. The young teacher has to have been telling the truth. The woman goes to the sink, fills the kettle and puts it onto the hook that hangs down over the fire.

I realise I haven't heard Jane say anything since they arrived back and when I look at her she is standing across from me looking really forlorn. She reminds me of one of those women I used to see when I was young, the ones who had been worn down with bullying men and poverty. I call her over and let her sit on my knee but she still says nothing, just cuddles close to me and I let her. I sit and wait as the woman finishes getting the table ready. I really need that cuppa and perhaps a decent explanation. After all Jane just might be exaggerating.

They lay on a lovely meal for us, homemade bread and some decent ham. The man and woman is what Jane has called them all the time. Now it's the only way I can think of them. The woman keeps herself busy and never once looks into my face. Whatever the man says, she never joins in and neither have any interaction with Jane. Jane doesn't even find anything to say to me which is unbelievable. I eat and drink my fill and listen to what the man has to say.

He tells me he has never hit the girls or threatened to throw Grace or Jane out of the bedroom window. I watch him and his wife as he says this. I also watch Jane whose eyes are huge and I know, because of her silence, he is lying. Jane must be very scared not to stick up for herself. She'll answer *me* back if she thinks she's right, even if she knows I'll smack her. I stand up when we've finished eating. I can hardly speak and just want to leave, I even feel threatened but can't say why. I feel very uncomfortable and know I'm taking Jane away from here.

"OK", I say, "I don't know what to say to you both. I just think that I would like you to get Jane's clothes, I am taking her with me". Jane comes over and stands quietly by me. Surprisingly, they say nothing. The woman leaves the room and comes back with a box, already packed.

The man picks the box up. "We're glad she's going", he says as he passes me Jane's coat. "We didn't want strange kids around us anyway, especially girls, at least a lad could have helped us out. One's enough to look after".

I don't say anything about what he says, I just want us to leave the house. "Here", I go to pick up the rag doll Mother made for Jane.

Jane refuses it, "No, it's not mine". I can see she doesn't want the doll, so place it back on the chair and walk out. The woman still says nothing and just opens the door, and we are almost thrown out.

CHAPTER SEVEN:
THE VICAR

Where we are heading, I have no idea. This is the middle of nowhere to me as we walk down the empty country road. Thank God it's fine and quite sunny although a bit of a breeze has come up, but we soon warm up as we seem to walk for rather a long time. Now she's left that place, Jane is skipping along beside me talking nine to the dozen, back to normal.

I ask her, "Why did you say that wasn't your doll? I would have made them give it to you".

She looks scared as if I was mad at her, "It was the baby's doll".

"No it wasn't, I saw your Nana making it and I wrapped it up for you".

"I giv' to it her, she's nice. Why are we walking so far, my legs are aching? Are we going to the train?" She moans on and on and I realise I really have no idea where we are.

Finally, I see an old couple in the garden of the first house we have seen since we set off down the road. It's a small cottage and the garden is the prettiest I've ever seen, it is like a picture painted by Gainsborough. Even the old dears in it match the beauty, they are about 70 years old and everything they wear says *country*. They have rosy complexions and she has her hair platted around her head. She is carrying a basket of flowers and wears a billowing cotton floral dress. If she had been wearing a bonnet she would have looked as if she had just walked out of one of the paintings. The man was wearing an old brown corduroy jacket, a heavy cotton shirt with a bright yellow cravat tucked into it, dark cream corduroy trousers and a Panama hat.

I call to them, "Excuse me, we are lost. Can you tell me where the bus stop is?"

Immediately the old lady comes over, "It's the other way dear, this way you'll come to the village, but there is another bus stop the other side of it".

The old man comes over, "Not from these parts, are you lass?"

"No, Jane is my daughter and has been evacuated here. I'm taking her away from where she was because I'm not sure they were very nice to her".

The old lady looks shocked, "Oh my dear child, are you alright?" She leans across the fence and lifts Jane's chin up to look at her. "How could anyone treat this little girl anyway but kindly?" She speaks as if she was from a different era. I feel as though I've stepped back in time.

Jane gives her one of her little girl smiles and says, "I'm OK now cos my Mam's taking me home". I don't tell her yet that it isn't convenient for me to take her home, that I have other plans and I'll be too busy. A few weeks ago, I got a job as a land girl on a farm and I've been asked to live in. I've been working there part-time these last few weeks and although it's hard, I absolutely love it. The girls I work with are great. I'm excited and looking forward to the change.

I get hold of her hand and say to the nice old couple, "Sorry, we have to go, I have to settle her in before I leave".

"Where did she stay?" the old lady asks.

I think I shouldn't say much as I want to leave her somewhere in the village. "Oh, just down the road at a farm, they just weren't very friendly".

They look at each other and he says, "Only one farm I know you could have walked from".

The old lady shakes her head, "Not the best of places. If we weren't so old I'd take her myself. Best thing you can do is to see the Vicar".

"Thanks very much", I reply, thinking if anyone knows someone who would take her, the Vicar would. "Could you tell me where he lives?"

"Big house t'other side of the village, just before the bus stop. It has mullioned windows so you can't miss it", the old gent says.

"Thank you", I say again as we leave and of course Jane has to wave at them until they are out of sight.

We can't miss the Vicarage, it's very imposing. Here, there is another lovely but much more formal garden in front of the house. I knock at the door using the huge iron knocker which is so loud it makes Jane jump. A very large man opens the door almost immediately and I can see by his dog collar that he is the Vicar. I put my hand out and he shakes mine then Jane's as I introduce us both. He looks how I think a Vicar should look: very pleasant, 50s, glasses and thinning hair. He is very well fed, I'm certain he's not missed a meal anytime during this rotten war. I start to explain what has happened as he ushers us through his front door. He waves me into a large sitting room, "Come in my dear, you look as though you could do with a cup of tea".

There it was again, that old fashioned courtesy, it reminds me of when I was young. Mother's family were very much the same when they came to visit us. Her sister lived in Biddston in Cheshire which is quite rural and posh. Having tea with them was important to Mother and she always made high tea when they visited using her best china tea set (the one that was my wedding present, now all destroyed in this damned war). The tea set always came out and a hand-embroidered tablecloth placed over the table. Mother made scones and opened a fresh jar of her own homemade strawberry jam, with fresh cream bought from the local dairy.

You had to take your own jug to the dairy to collect the cream and we could buy half a pint. One of us girls would be sent to collect it - usually me - but I didn't mind because I would sneak a sip or two before getting back home. There would be cakes on a three-tier cake-stand and if you were lucky, there would be Battenberg cake. I loved the coloured pieces in Battenberg but hated the almond paste that wrapped around it. I was never allowed it when Aunty Florrie visited because Mother told me it was rude to pick the paste off when visitors were round. I always thought Aunty Florrie was very posh because she always sipped her tea with her little finger sticking up. Of course, now I realise she was just affected.

The Vicar ushers us into a very formal sitting room and instructs us to sit down, pointing to a big leather settee. He then heads back towards the door and disappears though it, turning and saying "Excuse me, I will ask my housekeeper to make us some tea".

As we wait, I look around the room and it's so obvious that the war hasn't touched this village. The grand windows are clean, none broken or cracked. There is a fire blazing in the large, beautiful black iron grate, even though it isn't all that cold and he has electricity. I bet he doesn't even know that the baking of white bread is banned for now and that soap is rationed. I can't believe that this could be happening in 1942! It's as if we, the working class, are going backwards to Victorian times. This damned war is setting us back a century. I look around, thinking to myself that this house has a feeling of forever.

When the Vicar comes back in the room, he says, "There now, tea won't be long". He's no sooner said it than the door opens and an elderly woman bustles in, bringing a very welcome tray of tea, scones, fresh butter and jam. She sets the tray down as the Vicar says, "Thank you Mrs Spencer". She smiles, nods at us then leaves. He pours me a cup and gives Jane a glass of milk as we help ourselves to the scones.

When he sits down with his cup and scone in his hands, he says, "I'm Mr Miles so you can call me that instead of Vicar. Now, drink your tea and tell me your problems. What do I call you and this young lady?"

"I'm Elizabeth and this is my daughter Jane. I think you'll already know some of what I'm going to tell you because you're the same Vicar that visited the farm down the road". He looks surprised so I continue, "The farm boy who was sent away because of his 'you know what' with Grace".

He looks very uncomfortable, "Oh yes, very bad, very bad. Grace has gone home now I believe".

"Yes but Jane was living there as well". He looks surprised and goes to say something but I carry on talking, shaking my head at him, "She's OK, he didn't cuddle her but little girls have big ears". He catches on and realises I don't want to say any more in front of Jane.

He stands up and pulls a cord that's hanging on the wall, it's an old-fashioned bell! I look at him in amazement and say, "I didn't think those things were still in use". *Really!* I think it's awful that he can summon someone in this day and age with a servant's bell.

He smiles, "It still works but I only ever use it if it's important. I can assure you I would have to be very brave to pull that bell without good reason!"

Of course, it fascinates Jane. "Can I pull it," she asks.

"No you can't". Before I've finished Mrs Spencer comes through the door looking quite flustered.

"Is everything alright, Vicar?" She looks puzzled.

"Yes Mrs Spencer. I thought you might take Jane into the kitchen for a nice slice of your Victoria sandwich cake. Meanwhile, Elizabeth and I can have a little talk to each other".

Jane jumps up, she loves a fuss being made of her. "Can I ring the bell please?" She stands under the cord which is way too high for her to reach.

I start to say, "Don't be cheeky Jane", but it's too late, Mr Miles has already picked her up to pull the cord.

"Come on dear, I have to put some jam and cream on the cake and you can help me".

Jane grabs Mrs Spencer's hand and leaves without looking back. I think *that's what May said about kids soon forgetting* and feel relieved. I don't want to miss my chance to work on the farm. Mr Miles pours me a fresh cup of tea from the teapot, which is still hot because of a thick tea cosy over it. We start to talk. Jane and his housekeeper come back into the room carrying a large cake on a tray.

Mr Miles says, "Oh my dear, that was very quick! We haven't had our talk yet".

His housekeeper apologises, "I realise that but Jane really wanted her mother to see what she'd done and to have a piece of cake to eat right away".

Trust her to fuss but the cake does look delicious so I say, "I'd love a piece, then perhaps Jane could eat hers in the kitchen with you. We have a lot to sort out". Of course, Jane pulls a face but she does as she's told. After the Vicar and I have had a very large piece of cake served to us, they leave for the kitchen.

As we eat our cake I say, "It's getting late and as there is only one more bus leaving at 7 tonight so we better talk".

He leans forward, "I had hoped the problem had sorted itself out when the boy was sent home".

"I don't think so. Those children were bullied and frightened by the man who owned the farm". I am really annoyed and tell him everything. He sits quietly and lets me rant on.

He says, "It's wartime my dear and everything is a mess, what can we do about it? I think it was a first time for the boy and he was ashamed. His mother came to take him home. I think it must have taught him a very hard lesson".

I look at Mr Miles and think in a way he's probably right, the boy should have learnt his lesson. His mother had been told and I bet his father is away in one of the services. They are probably decent people and I'm sure life won't be easy for him for some time to come. The farmers need so much help, they probably won't take any other kids. And last but not least, I still have to find someone to take Jane in and it is getting late.

"You are right" I say, "I just want Jane to go to someone who'll take care of her. It's too dangerous to take her back home, we're still getting Blitzed even though it isn't every night now". I realise I have to move fast, I don't want to miss that last bus to the train station.

"Well my dear, what do you want me to do?" The Vicar looks concerned and I explain I want him to help me find someone to take Jane in. He stands up, "You're very lucky. I know a young mother who I think would be glad of Jane's company. We'll have to go right away if you need to get that bus".

He goes out of the room and returns with Jane in tow. I am so relieved. He takes us for a short walk down the same road we had walked up to find the Vicarage earlier. We then turn right down a path where there is a row of five cottages facing a small stream. It really is very pretty and peaceful. I feel quite sad when I think about the terrible condition of our poor town. Mr Miles knocks the door of the second cottage along and a young woman opens it. He introduces us and after some explaining about my position, he leaves telling us he has other business to attend to. Looking at him, I think it's probably another piece of Mrs Spencer's Victoria sponge.

'Helen' introduces herself and asks us in. She makes us a cup of tea and we talk about Jane, who she seems glad to be taking in. She tells me she's 19 and her husband is a lieutenant in the Royal Navy. She'd married him at age 18 by special license because he'd been called up to leave on his ship almost immediately. They knew the dangers he would face and wanted to feel they belonged to each other. They only had the one night together before he'd had to leave and she had conceived on that night. She laughed when she told me it was a honeymoon baby. I thought, *some honeymoon*. Her baby girl is about six months old now and so pretty, she looks very much like her mam.

Helen tells me she is very lonely. She'd originally moved to the village to be near her mother-in-law who wasn't too well at the time, but things went from bad to worse and her mother-in-law died suddenly just after the baby was born. Now she really was on her own, although her neighbours were very caring and did keep an eye on her and the baby. So she would love to have Jane for company. I can't believe how lucky I am, not only is Jane is going to be OK, I seem to be doing Helen a favour leaving her there. I can now leave Jane without any worries about her wanting to go home.

It turned out that Helen's husband's ship had been in port for repairs when his mother died. He was allowed compassionate leave for the funeral. It also meant he was able to see his daughter for the first time. When he left for his ship, Helen's parents had wanted her to move back to their area to be near them. Nevertheless, Helen told me this is the home where she and husband have spent their married life so far and she wanted him to be able to see it in his thoughts of home.

I hope he is lucky and gets home, the Germans have a large fleet of submarines that have sunk so many of our ships. I finish my tea and get up to leave. Jane jumps up. "Sit down, you're staying with Helen", I say and hurriedly say goodbye to dash for the bus. I feel a sense of relief. Jane will be all right there and I haven't missed my bus.

CHAPTER EIGHT:
HOMECOMING

I'm now a 'land girl' and really happy, it's the best job I've ever had. The gang of girls I work with are a smashing crowd.

I was originally offered a chance to work as a forestry worker but was warned not to take it. One of Mother's neighbours came in to have a cuppa with her and Mother told her about the job. Her neighbour told her how hard and rough it is, she has a niece who does it and because she's a single girl, she's had to take it. It's in a forest near the farm I work at and I've seen for myself how hard that job is. The girls have to do what big strapping men used to do, they call them *Timber Jill's*. Luckily, I was allowed to turn it down because of the kids.

I'm working on a farm with half a dozen other girls and it's the hardest work most of us have ever had to do. Everyone is fit and slim except for Maggie who's a big, well built, bouncy, beautiful girl and one of the best. She tells us she has a gland problem but if anyone of us leaves something on our plates, she'll polish it off.

Out in the fields we sing all day and have a great laugh especially when Peter the farmer isn't around. In fact, it's mostly him we laugh about; he's in his early 50s, looks 60 and thinks he's the cat's whiskers. He's a bachelor and wants a wife. The poor man should realise if he hasn't managed to get one by now, there must be a reason. We are a bit mean really, he isn't a bad boss. We have heard there are some very mean farmers who don't treat the girls well at all. Some of their wives are even worse, they're really nasty to them and make their lives quite miserable. It's cruel the way some are treated. The new girls are always given the hoeing to do which is tiring and backbreaking work. It's real drudgery so we try to do it together as a group. We sing and have as much fun and laughter as we can while we're working. It helps the time to pass more quickly.

Peter makes sure we have good food and keeps the fire in the kitchen going all day. Most of the cooking and baking is done on the huge range, and with so many girls living in the house, it's in use all the time. The house is old and very well built with thick stone walls.

So it's always cool in the kitchen if the fire goes out but it isn't very often, even in the summer. When we come in cold or wet, we are always able to warm ourselves up and dry our clothes overnight. Peter makes a good job keeping the fire going, I think we should be a bit kinder to him. Poor Peter! He's so homely, he certainly was the last in the queue when God gave looks out. Such a strange fella. Maggie is kind, she often says, "Poor Peter, I'm sure he could scrub up well". I'm afraid I think only a mother could love him.

Once a month I have a Sunday off and I'm supposed to go home to see Mother, Dad and the kids. They expect me to come home to see them every time but I'm ashamed to say I make excuses. I tell them I have to work extra Sundays because we are short of staff. I just love being here. When I do go home, I return very early on the Monday morning on what they call the 'milk train'; I must admit I just can't wait to get back to the farm. When I'm here, life with the lasses is great.

The local village hall has a dance on Saturday night every week. Most of the girls from the farms around here go and it's great fun. Three of us girls from our farm go as often as we can. Two of the other girls from our farm have to go home every weekend as they have older parents who need their help, it's a shame because we have such a good time. Thankfully mine are quite fit and don't need my help. I treat them when I do see them, taking Mother butter and bacon and giving Dad a shilling now and again, that keeps him happy.

The Saturdays I'm at the farm are the days I look forward to the most. We love dressing up in our best clothes. It's a hell of a job getting ready together but we help each other. We have to keep filling the huge kettle and pans that sit on the range to keep the large tin bath full and hot. We all share the same block of Sunlight or Lifebuoy soap. They both sting my eyes so I don't use much on my face. I'm lucky, Mother managed to get me some Pond's Face Cream for my birthday so I clean it with that. Now soap is rationed, we girls all share with each other.

I think about my Tom, I used to have to use a lot of soap on him. Even scrubbing his knees with the scrubbing brush didn't always get them really clean. I hope he's being kept clean on the farm. I realise it's about time I went to see them, it's just making the time, I'm so busy.

Saturday is the one night poor Peter is locked out of his own kitchen for over an hour. There isn't a lock on the door but we now put a heavy chair under the handle. What happened was that on the first Saturday we organised our bath, there were five near naked women in the kitchen. We didn't think that after warning Peter not to come in that he would. He did! Pretending to be all innocent and shocked, he stood there for what seemed a few minutes apologising and taking everything in. We'd grabbed whatever we could to cover ourselves. Not Maggie though, she was standing there in her vest and knickers, which was more than most of us were wearing. When we all squealed, he stood there still pretending to apologise.

"I forgot", he said, eyes popping out and almost drooling.

Maggie walked over to him, "Well," she said, "I'll remind you". She picked him up and threw him out. We went into hysterics, laughing at his shocked but lecherous face.

Maggie said, "That'll keep him happy in bed for a long time, the old perv'".

When we come out of the kitchen, poor Peter is nowhere to be seen; we don't even see him as we leave. It's a nice night so we walk to the hall. He usually drops us off but we decide to leave him in peace tonight, wherever he is hiding. Tomorrow though, we will be hard on him because although we aren't really mad at him; it'll be fun giving him a tough time.

We arrive at the hall and pay our sixpence entrance fee. Because we've walked there tonight, it's a bit later and the hall is already bouncing. There are a few local single men and women, and one or two couples from the surrounding area who also come to the dance. The men are friendly but most of the women seem to look down on us. Woe betide us if one of their men asks us to dance.

Everyone is having fun, we all think we could be dead tomorrow. How do we know when life is ever going to be normal again? Now the Americans have joined the war, we have some of their guys over here. There is a military camp at the nearby village of

Flookburgh, and some of them come to visit our town. There's a girl who works in a Co-op at home, she's met an American from the camp and they're the talk of the town. Mostly because every one of the girls are jealous to death, including Bella and if I admit it, me. We have been told he's a film star. We already know that Clark Gable has been to the Roxy but he was on his own. Well at least, he didn't have any women with him! He was sneaked in when the lights went out and left before the lights came on again. I only know this because a friend has a mate who works there as an usherette, and she told her. Of course, she was told she hadn't to tell anyone so naturally most of the town know.

Figure 15 - Flookburgh Village Square

However, Bella came rushing in the night before I came back here and told me, "You won't believe it. Last night at the Roxy, that lass was there with her Yank. You won't believe who he is".

"Who is he?" I ask.

"Guess, go on, guess!" she's all excited.

"How can I guess you ninny?" I shake my head and laugh, "Just tell me".

"I'll give you a clue, he's always a baddie in his films". Now she was getting on my nerves.

"Forget it", I tell her. She's still a daft young girl and drives me dotty at times.

"Steve Cochran, that's who! Steve Cochran! I don't like him, he's a gangster".

I explain, "No Bella, he's a film star, a gangster is what he pretends to be in the films he makes".

She looks at me, "Oh yes I never thought of it like that. I like him now". I just laugh at her and wish I were still that young and daft.

Luckily the dance we go to is full of GIs. They are from another camp about two miles away and so far they don't seem to have any celebrities. Most of them are young and good looking so the girls are quite happy.

The best thing for me is most of them are great at jiving. The band is good considering they are all local musicians, the saxophonist and trumpet player are as good as the those in the Glenn Miller Orchestra. When they play the *Chattanooga Choo Choo*, they do such a good job that the place goes wild and we girls are thrown over shoulders and through legs. We jive until we can hardly draw breath. When we finally stop, we go over to the table to get a drink. There isn't much choice, just the usual orange cordial or tea. The sixpence entrance fee is for the local church and whilst we don't mind paying the tanner to come in, we all complain that tuppence a drink is too much, and it's so weak. But it's a great place for us to let our hair down and I love it. It's so much fun having the chance to dance with the boys, we forget all about the war and our various worries, and have a great time.

Until one Saturday that is, when I thought I might have to stop going. Most of the American boys are friendly, great fun and very polite. Except one particular GI Sergeant who's very pushy and tries to get me to dance with him all the time. He's different to most of the others and I feel quite repulsed by him. He's the kind of man you wouldn't like to meet if you were on your own in the dark. But because he's an American serviceman a long way from home, I feel mean thinking like that, so I'm polite and have a dance with him at least once on the night. It's always uncomfortable, he pulls me to him and I feel embarrassed as he tries to fondle me in a very nasty way.

At the end of the night, the band always play a romantic slow tune and they're good. By now, a lot of the girls from the other farms have started to see some of the young GIs so there's a lot of romance in the air. This Saturday night they played Glenn Miller's *Perfidia*. I love it and although I haven't a special partner, I always enjoy the slow sensuous foxtrot.

This night is different. The Sergeant comes over and tries to get me to dance with him as usual. I refuse very politely and he still tries to pull me onto the floor but I won't go, so he starts calling me a slut and a whore. By now I'm upset and mortified, as well as afraid. A stranger comes up and pushes him away from me, but the Yank comes back and tries to hit him. The stranger just gives him one punch on the chin and he goes down. By now, the music has stopped and everyone is watching. I'm scared because the American boys look after each other. There's a silence and then I start to apologise to everyone. Two of the American boys come over to pick him up.

One says, "Sorry Ma'am, Sarg' isn't the nicest of guys. We'll take him back to camp and make sure he doesn't come here again".

A lieutenant comes over and turns to the crowd, "You won't see him again, I'll make sure of that. On behalf of the boys, I hope you won't hold this against us. We all have a good time when we come over here and you have made us so welcome. It helps the young ones who miss home so much".

One of the older local men - who run the hall and dance - walks over and shakes the lieutenant's hand. "You're OK lad, don't thee worry, you're a grand lot and we really appreciate all you've done for our village. There are bad apples everywhere. We'll look forward to seeing you all next week".

Then the lieutenant comes over to where me and the stranger who'd knocked down the sergeant, are standing. He holds his hand out to the young man and they shake hands.

"Thanks, you did the right thing". As he stands shaking the stranger's hand, he turns to me and smiles, "I'm sorry Elizabeth, it won't ever happen again".

The stranger smiles at the lieutenant and myself. He speaks in slightly halting English, as if he has to think about what he is saying. "It is OK, he shouldn't have insulted any of these decent young women here. You did the right thing taking him away".

I am taking it all in, although I feel in a slight daze. The stranger who came to my rescue has an odd accent. He can't be a prisoner of war, the Italian prisoners have softer accents than that plus they're not allowed out anyway. His accent is more like the German prisoners', just less harsh and he speaks quietly. I'm very confused, he can't be one of them either as they also aren't allowed to leave the camp except for when they work on the local farms.

The lieutenant looks as surprised as I am, "You don't come from around these parts do you?"

"No I am half-Polish, my mother is Irish," he replies carefully. "I escaped to Britain with my family two days before the Germans invaded Poland, my father is a Jew. When we arrived here in Britain, because I was an aircraft cadet I was able to join and train with the British Air Force immediately and flew as a gunner until I was wounded".

I realise he must only be about 22-23 years old and he's already in the middle of the conflict. The lieutenant holds out his hand again. "Welcome to our war, sir, you do a wonderful job. The young British airmen, including yourself and your brothers of course, are the bravest we have ever met. Now our boys have come in, I'm sure they'll be the same. I guess you're on leave, when do you go back?"

The stranger patted his left leg. "My foot almost lost it. A wonderful surgeon managed to put it back together, just lost a couple of toes. I am recuperating and helping out at Manor Farm for now".

The lieutenant pulls a face and shakes his head in sympathy, "I'm sorry, it's hard on you. Let's get together at the local on

Tuesday night. I would be proud to buy you a drink". He laughed, "If they have anything in to drink that is. Are you a warm beer man?"

The stranger hesitates over some of his words again but he is very literate. "Yes I am. The saying is, when in Rome do as the Romans do. I would be proud to have a drink with you boys. I can't get away until 7 o'clock, is that OK?"

The lieutenant nodded, "See you then". He turned and made for the door. Most of the dancers had left and I could see the old men who ran the hall were waiting to lock up.

"Thank you again," I say, looking properly at the stranger for the first time.

He takes my hand and smiles, "How could I not help a lady like you, when she is in distress?" When he smiles and looks down at me, I see beautiful blue-grey eyes. I realise he must be the most good-looking man I've ever seen. My heart almost stops with the shock I feel.

I stare at him, completely breathless and know I just can't speak. He looks concerned, "It's obvious you have had a shock. Come outside and get some air".

I realise I am still staring at him, "Yes I've had a shock", I reply. He holds my arm as we walk through the door. I feel a thrill shoot through my body and I take a deep breath as I wonder what on earth is happening to me? I move away from him, "I'm OK now really, I have to find my friends".

He says, "I think we are the only two left here Elizabeth". The way he says my name makes me shiver, it's like a caress.

I look at him and ask, "How do you know my name?" I feel breathless again.

"The lieutenant called you Elizabeth", he answers. Of course, he'd remember the lieutenant saying it to me. I look around and realise it is very dark, even the hall lights are out now.

All I can say is, "Oh of course he did". I don't really like the dark but think to myself if I set off now I might catch up with the girls.

I hold my hand out once more, "Goodbye and thank you once again". He catches my hand and kind of bows as he kisses it. There it goes again, what on earth is happening to my heart?

"My name is Ludvik but most people call me Ludo. I would like you to call me that if you would. I will walk with you to see you get home safely".

Knowing how scared I will be, I hesitate, "Hh-mm I'll be alright, really".

He laughs again, "I'm sure you would be but I'm going past where you work on my way back to Manor Farm".

I'm embarrassed, "Of course I wasn't thinking, thank you".

We set off and I realise I'm really glad he is there. There are howls and rustling going on all around us as we walk along the path. I would have been scared to death on my own. He sees me jump as an owl lets out a screech and puts his hand into mine. I feel my heart flutter and beat hard again, just a touch is enough. I think to myself, *what am I going to do?* If just a touch sets me off, I also shiver in delicious anticipation. The thought of more both excites and scares me. I realise he's trying to reassure me all the time I'm thinking these thoughts. I flush and I am so glad he can't see me properly in this light. Then I hear what he's saying and I'm ashamed.

"There's nothing here to worry about," he says. "Remember how lovely it is in the daylight, I love it. The peace here has really helped me to get better. I've lost many of my friends in the raids and so quickly. This damned war. At first, I felt really guilty that it hadn't happened to me". He slapped his leg as if he hated it, "I've got off easy". For the first time, I notice his limping. I feel like crying as I hear the strain and sadness in his voice.

"I'm sorry," I say. He squeezes my hand and I tell him, "You'll be OK here, it's a great place to recuperate in peace". I feel guilty, knowing how much he must be going through and now I've caused him more problems. We've reached the farm and he's still holding my hand. I don't want him to let it go, I don't know what to do. We stand for what seems like several minutes then he bends his head and kisses me. I love it. He gently kisses my mouth, my cheeks, the tip of my nose, then my lips again. Now I know what they mean when I read my romantic novels and the heroine says she feels like she's drowning.

This shouldn't be happening, I push him away, "I'm sorry, sorry, I'm married. I really must go". I look up at him again. "Please", I want him to leave because I know I can't.

He pulls me to him again, "Good night Elizabeth", and kisses me for a second time before walking away. I lift the latch on the kitchen door, walk into the farmhouse and know I'm not going to sleep much tonight.

5 o'clock comes too soon. I wash my face in cold water and go down to breakfast, the girls all looking at me as I sit down. I can feel their eyes on me, waiting. I pour myself a cup of tea and butter my toast, saying nothing.

"Oh yes, where were you last night?" Maggie laughs, "You don't look as if you've had much sleep. Who is he? Never seen him before and looking like he does, I would remember".

"I came home on my own, you lot left me," I don't want to tell them how I feel. I just want to hug this feeling to myself. I have to forget last night, he did walk away so might not have felt the same as I do. I know if he had asked to stay longer, I might not have been able to refuse him. Questions fly around in my mind and I wonder if he'll be at the dance next Saturday. Would he ignore me or just be friendly? I know what I want and know it is wrong. I should have been home but we'd volunteered to work this Sunday. Most of the girls stayed as we've got behind with the haymaking and cleaning the place up.

It's late afternoon and Maggie and me are working in the farmyard, I bend down to shovel some cow muck up. Maggie digs me in the ribs. "See who's at the gate?" she laughs. I don't look up or speak, the smell of the muck is horrible and I want to make sure I get it all on the shovel and not on *me*. I've no idea who she is talking about. I mutter, trying not to inhale the smell, "I'm not looking until I've put this dollop into the wheelbarrow". I struggle to carry the shovelful across to the barrow, put it in and knock the shovel on the edge. Then I look over to see who Maggie has said was here.

"Oh my God, it's Ludo. I've just walked across the yard bent like a hunchback with a shovelful of cow s--- to put into the barrow. You bitch! Why didn't you tell me?"

She laughs her whole body shaking, "I did and you ignored me".

I feel my face getting hot and red just as I did as a teenager. He is leaning on the farmyard gate, trying not to laugh. I walk over with my head up in the air, trying to look a little less silly and hoping I look cool and confident.

"Hello Elizabeth, I was passing and noticed you two girls in the yard". He looks just as handsome now as he did last night and my heart misses a beat again.

I am mortified, "I didn't realise it was you when Maggie said".

Maggie calls over, "It'll teach you to listen to me in future. I'm going to put kettle on". Gesturing, she asks Ludo, "Would you like a cuppa, sunshine?"

He smiles back at Maggie, "No thank you, I have to get back, I just want a moment to ask Elizabeth something".

He takes a very white hanky out of his pocket, leans over and wipes my face and I see what has to be a stain of cow muck on it. I can feel my face flaming again. He holds my face, stares into my eyes and I feel I'm going to die with embarrassment. "You are beautiful Elizabeth", he smiles, "even with farmyard manure on your face". That makes me laugh! *Beautiful?* I think he must be shortsighted. I can't think of a thing to say in response and wonder what on earth he wants to ask. There's a silence and he looks a bit uncomfortable. "I didn't tell you the truth. I wasn't just passing the farm, I went to see if you were in the fields and one of the girls said you were working here today. Elizabeth, can we meet somewhere tonight to talk? I haven't been able to think about anything else since I kissed you".

As I listen to him, all I can think about is how I want to kiss his mouth again. I try to think where we could meet, I'm not sure we should be seen together on our own.

I say, "I don't know where we could meet. I really don't think it would be sensible to give the gossips something to talk about. I am married you know". Oh how I want to see him so much. To be alone with him – but common sense tells me we shouldn't meet. Then I think to myself, *who would know? There is a war on; no one knows what might happen tomorrow. We might not live to see another day.*

He tells me, "I live in the Lodge at the end of the Manor House drive". He gets hold of my hand, "We could go there if you like?"

I pull my hand away, "No, do you think I'm that sort of woman?"

"I'm sorry. Sorry Elizabeth, I promise I just want us to talk. To get to know one another. Whatever is happening to me, I know is happening to you too". He looks so unhappy and he's right. This rush of emotion I feel is like nothing that has ever happened to me before, and I ache to touch him. I loved Fred very much when we married but this is different and I have grown up so much since then.

"Alright, I do believe you and I know we need to talk about it. I can't get any time off until Saturday night; maybe we could leave the dance early?" I didn't know then, that I wouldn't be at the dance again the next weekend.

Figure 16 – 'Women's Land Army' Posters

CHAPTER NINE:
IS IT LOVE?

It's Monday morning, and I'm at Barrow Central railway station waiting to catch the 5.30am train back to the farm. I can't wait to get back, even the extra days off I was given have meant nothing to me, given the reason for my unexpected trip.

I'm back in time to see the others leaving for work. Every one of the girls gives me a kiss and a hug as they go. It's ploughing and planting season out in the fields, and it's hard work. I notice a couple of the younger ones look worn out. I have to change into my overalls before I start work so climb the stairs to the bedroom. Maggie wasn't in the kitchen when I arrived back but one of the girls told me she was staying behind at the house. When I come back downstairs and into the kitchen, Maggie is sitting at the table.

Seeing me, she jumps up and gives me a big hug. "I've missed you girl, how's the lad? Was it bad? Did you kill anyone? You and me are staying here to work today".

I laugh at her as I untangle myself from her bear hug. "One question at a time! I've missed you and everyone here too. Tom's OK now he's back at home but he's going to have to be built-up for a few months, just to get him back to his normal self. Yes it was bad, broke my heart when I saw him but no I didn't kill anyone, there was no-one there as they kept out of my way". I pause, then say, "After the war---", my chest contracts with anger, "---I have sworn to myself that I'm going back with a gun to shoot all three of them".

I've had to make an emergency trip to see our Tom and was outraged at the state he was in: weak, thin and pale. Miss Anderson, our Jane's previous guardian, had recently taken Jane to visit him as a treat and shortly afterwards I received a letter from her saying she thought he was being badly neglected, starved and used for cheap labour. I collected him as soon as I could after that.

I feel upset again thinking about it and a bit guilty at leaving Jane with yet more strangers. Still I know she's with good people, they'd even sent for the local nurse while I was there to clean her head up as it turned out she had nits! Maggie goes to hug me again but I dodge her large arms and laugh.

"I'm OK, just want to get back to normal. I'm so glad to be back. Just need a cuppa before I start work".

Maggie pours me a cup of tea, "I know someone who'll be very glad you're back. You should have seen the look on his face when you weren't there on Saturday night. He came over to me and asked if you were sick. His face was drained, I thought if anyone was sick it was him". She laughed, "*Love*sick that is, poor Ludo. I told him what had happened but of course I wasn't sure when - or even if - you would be back. I offered myself in your place, the look of horror on his face was almost comical". She laughed so much at her own joke, her bosom was heaving up and down at least three inches. "Poor lad was so embarrassed! I let him know I was only joking. I don't know what's going to happen with you two but I think sparks are going to fly".

I know what she means but have no idea what Ludo or I can do about it. "How can anything happen, Maggie? I'm married, I'm several years older than him and he's a boy!" I moan. I'm nearly crying by this time and lean on Maggie's chest, "Oh Maggie, I don't know what's happening".

She pats my back, "Go with the swing girl. If it's meant to be, it'll happen. If you want my advice, I think you should go with your feelings. This war has changed things. Life will never be the same and who knows what's around the corner?" She starts to laugh again, "And anyway, how the hell are you going to turn a man like him down? This is someone who has everything, he might be younger than you but he is quite obviously a man *not* a boy. Now we have to get to work before our dear boss tells us off".

I get up and swill my face under the kitchen tap. The shock of the cold water makes me feel better. I clear the table and tidy the kitchen with Maggie's help, then we leave to feed the pigs. It makes life feel a bit more normal to me. News travels quickly in the farming community so at lunchtime whilst Maggie and I are eating in the kitchen, there's a knock at the door. Maggie's naturally nosy so is usually first up to answer it but now she sits supping her tea, signaling for me to answer it. I get up and hesitantly open the door, the way she's behaving has let me know he would be standing there.

"Ludo!" I almost throw myself at him. Or was it him who drew me to him? Whatever. I was in his arms and we were kissing. I start to cry.

He pushes me away but stands with his hands holding my arms, "I'm sorry Elizabeth." Then he repeats, "Elizabeth?"

I look at his face and know nothing is going to stop what we are feeling. I answer, "What?"

He pulls me back to him, "Nothing, I just want to say your name again and again". We both look at Maggie, who's stood transfixed.

She says, "Bloody hell". Shakes her head and passes us as she walks out through the open door. She doesn't even look at us again as she tells me, "Go in, shut the door and I'll cover for you if anyone asks".

We go into the kitchen and close the door. We both stand there, looking at each other. There is an awkward silence. Ludo gets hold of my hand and guides me to the huge old sofa. We sit down facing each other and both go to speak at once. Ludo gently puts his finger on my lips, "We have to talk". Even the feel of his fingers on my lips sends a delicious shiver through me. I think this thing between us is bigger than both of us.

I ask him, "What's happening to us Ludo?" I shake my head.

He smiles and gets holds of my hand. "This feeling I have for you, I've never felt before". He puts my hand to his mouth again and kisses it gently, "I love you Elizabeth. I know I always will".

My heart almost stops again, I am so shocked with happiness.

"I love you too Ludo but I'm a wife, mother and several years older than you. It can't happen".

He holds my face and stares straight into my eyes. "Look at me, tell me it can't happen". I know I cannot do it so just shake my head. He smiles and says, "It has happened and we can't lose it".

I need to think so decide to make a drink. Putting his hands gently down from my face, I stand up and start to fill the kettle. Whilst I'm messing with the teacups, Ludo comes over and sits at the table. He pulls me down onto his knee, "I know we need to be careful and I have to leave now. Still we should talk. Please come to the Lodge tonight if you can. I promise I will bring you back to the farm when we've settled this".

I stand up away from him and pour the tea, "I can't, I have to make up for being off these last few days, we are working late all week". I know I need some time to think. "I'll see you at the dance on Saturday and talk then I promise". I stroke his precious face, "I know what we have is special and we need to sort it out".

We sit quietly drinking our tea. He stands, walks over and draws me to him again. "A few days. I can wait a few days. I think". He kisses me gently then with great passion.   After that, he sits me back down on the chair and leaves. I'm confused, I want him so much. How can we ever get together?

I can't wait for Saturday and the rest of the week drags by. The girls give me a hard time, joking all the time. I keep them guessing. Maggie is the only one who really knows there is more than a little something between us. She's a great friend so she promises not to tell the girls more than they already think they know.

I see Ludo drive past the big house in the jeep every day. He seems to have to go past wherever we are working and gives us all a wave. I wave nonchalantly at him. Then I have to listen to the girls as they talk about trying to get off with him at the dance, I even join in with them. Maggie makes the most of knowing something the others don't and keeps on about being the first to catch him. I laugh with them, all the time feeling my heart beating so hard in my chest and a delicious feeling of passion, fear and apprehension whenever I see him. It must have been the longest week I've ever had, even longer than the month I used to have to wait to meet Fred, but that might have been because he didn't pass by every day. Now I stop myself thinking about Fred because I don't think he cares about us anymore.

It's Saturday at last but alas, I've had to go home again. Mother got a message to me on Friday saying that I had to get home or Dad would come and fetch me. I never even had time to see Ludo. I think we aren't ever meant to be, perhaps it's a warning. Maggie is going to let him know what has happened. When I arrive home, Mother has arranged for me to go to collect Jane from the Everest's house in the country. She'd received a letter addressed to me and had opened it. It was from Major Everest asking why I hadn't come to collect Jane as he'd requested. Mother and Dad both go on and on at me, telling me I have to bring her home now that the Blitz has really slowed down, there are very few air raids now and I've run out of excuses. They are really mad at me and Dad's accusing me of having too good a time.

Dad looks at me, "I can see just by looking at you that's something's going on. I've heard about the Yanks coming to the dance near the farm. Look at you, done up to the eyebrows, don't tell me it isn't for someone's benefit".

I feel my face flaming but I know I can swear that I'm not seeing a Yank. "Dad, I can swear on the kids' lives I'm not messing about with the Yanks".

He shouts, "I'm not daft, there's *something* going on, is it the farmer?"

Again I know I can answer truthfully, "What an insult! You should see him, he's a real hayseed, not my type at all".

He says, "I don't care what you say, something is going on. I might be deaf but I'm not daft". He threatens to tell Fred when he comes home. I'm mad at him because he is only guessing, they know nothing at all about Ludo and me. Dad has no reason to accuse me. Still, I realise I have to do as they say so decide I'm really going to have to bring Jane home.

Mother's friend's husband has a car so she's paid him to take me to pick up Jane on Sunday morning. Mother has decided to come with us as she's really looking forward to seeing Jane. I tell her to stay in the car when we get there. I don't want her talking to the Everests so I tell her Mrs Everest is too sick for visitors.

As it is, I don't see them myself. They have left Jane with the housekeeper. She is her usual fussy self and throws her arms around me. Then calls me "Mummy", I soon put her right about that! We say a quick goodbye to the housekeeper as Jane can't wait to see Mother when I tell her she is in the car. They sit together in the back of the car. As I listen to the fuss Mother is making of her, I decide I have done the right thing. At least I won't have any more trouble with her moving again. Now I can't wait for tomorrow morning.

CHAPTER TEN:
MY NEEDS

Although it's hard for my mother and I know I'm being selfish, I desperately need some time with Ludo. Day or night, I cannot think of anything else. I feel as though my brain is going to explode. So as we get dinner ready in the scullery, I tell mother I have to work through next Sunday because we are so busy.

She is angry with me and says she's telling Dad as soon as he comes in. I had thought she wouldn't tell him until next weekend but I know she's finding two kids hard to look after. If it had just been our Tom, she would manage fine - I know he's mischievous but it was OK until Jane came home. Mother blames Tom but Jane's such a whiner, she probably never gives them any peace. I know at this point I have to give in and agree with whatever Mother tells me I have to do.

I ask Mother not to say anything until we've eaten our Sunday dinner. Dad will be more content after that and I think perhaps I can talk him round. Also the kids can go out to play when we've finished eating, Jane listens in on everything we adults talk about and I don't want her whining about wanting me to come home in front of them. I go cold when I hear Dad coming up the lobby. I feel as if he will see the truth in my eyes. I have to look for excuses and suddenly realise I'm really lying to them both for the first time in my life. The worst of it is, I want to.

Mother and me make small talk whilst eating dinner. I usually enjoy this meal but right now I feel like I'm chewing cardboard. Dad is only interested in his dinner, he's so deaf he doesn't join in with the conversation. He's had a couple of beers at the pub with his mates and usually goes to sleep straight after eating.

When we've finished, I get the kids to put their coats on and send them back home telling them they can play out for a couple of hours before bedtime. Of course, Jane moans and wants to stay until I tell her she can have a couple of her friends in the house to play and she's off like a shot! I go out to the scullery when they leave to make a pot of tea. When I come back into the kitchen, Mother, Dad and me sit at the table drinking our tea and saying nothing. Then Mother gets up from the table and heads for the scullery, taking her unfinished cup of tea with her.

As she leaves, she tells me, "I'm going to wash up, you tell him what you've told me". I slice another piece off the Victoria sponge I'd made before I left the farm and pass it to Dad. I watch him take a large bite and wait. He takes a great swig of tea and says, "Aye that's good. Thanks lass, you can meck a good cake".

I smile at him, "It's a good job I've got the job at the farm".

"Aye about that", he says, "That's why we've made you come home today. Time you packed it in, the kids need you here. They're far too much work for your mother to manage now".

I pass him a shilling, "I was going to give you this next week out of my extra pay".

He shoves it back at me and roars, "What extra pay?"

He looks so angry I flinch and feel my face flame. "I have to work next weekend, they're shorthanded".

He glares at me and shakes his head, "I've told you to get home to these kids. Tom's running wild and Jane's fretting, they are both unsettled. They need you home now".

I know I've lost but I have to buy some time to see Ludo, I push the bob back. "OK I'll put my notice in but I have to work a month's notice. I can't leave until then as it's a bad time, they're so busy". I hope he believes me, I know I could leave in a week because of my family position. Nevertheless, I have at least to finish what I might have started with Ludo.

Mother comes in and looks at me as if she knows what I'm up to. She says quietly, "I heard everything; you've shocked me, trying to bribe your Dad like that".

I bluster, "I've an extra two and six for you. It was a surprise, I just wanted to show you how grateful I am that you have looked after the kids so well".

Mother takes the half-crown I offer, "I'll have it anyway", she says, "but it will be to buy wool for the kid's winter jumper, I've saved my coupons for them. Now I know something is going on and you look terrible, I can tell it's bothering you. I really hope it isn't one of those Yanks up there".

I feel tears running down my face, "Mother I promise you it isn't a Yank and I will sort it out in the next month". I know I am telling the truth, it does have to be sorted. The problem is I know how much I want it to go the wrong way. But I have to face it, I have fallen in love so hard and I have to follow it up. I decide not to dwell on the future. Mother has realised how upset I am and I see a little sympathy in her eyes. She leans over and pats my hand. I glance over at Dad but he's dozed off. I'm relieved.

She says, "I know Fred's not the best husband love, but he's a lot better than most. He did take care of you until he left".

I cry and say, "Yes I know but he left us and I've *had* to work. He doesn't keep in touch, he even went to Ireland and Liverpool on his few leave times instead of coming home".

Mother looks shocked, "How do you know that?"

I explain, "His sister told me quite innocently. I feel that he has deserted us and I can't forgive him". Mother looks shocked at what I've told her, I can see she is really sorry for me now.

"Love, he's your husband, it will sort itself out when he gets home".

I don't believe her and don't know how to answer. After all, what am I hoping to do? I get up. "I have to get home, the kids need their bath". On my Sundays off, I bathe them at home and let them sleep with me. We have to get up at 5am so that I can drop them off at Mother's house then I leave to get the train back to the farm.

The next morning as I leave, I say, "See you soon". Better they don't know I'm not coming home next Sunday. I sit quietly on the train. Not looking around because it is full of girls going back to farms. I know a lot of them from the Saturday dance. I'm deep in my own thoughts, I feel awful and completely drained. Falling in love can have terrible consequences.

With a start I realise the train has pulled into my station near the farm. I pick up my attaché case and feel so weak; it feels as heavy as if it's packed with iron weights. I step off the train, thinking I won't be doing this for much longer. My heart falls into my boots. It isn't just because of Ludo, I love my job here and get on really well with all the girls. Also, I have made the best of friends with Maggie and life won't be the same without her. I walk up the platform not looking around. I know I'm struggling to hold tears back and don't want to see anyone who would know me.

I'm almost at the entrance when someone gently touches my shoulder. I dread turning around, one kind word would bring everything I'm feeling to a head. I carry on walking through the entrance, ignoring the touch. As I get to a quiet corner, I turn to see who it could be, thinking it might be Maggie. Which was a daft thought really because if it had have been her, I would have known as I would already have been in one of her huge bear hugs. I'll miss her so, she's so much fun and such a good sort.

When I do turn to look, my heart almost stops: it's Ludo. I feel faint and stagger a little, he catches me and holds me to him. I push away from him, looking around. Luckily the few passengers who had arrived and alighted with me have already gone. Fortunately for us, it's a tiny station and there are only two permanent station staff who are busy elsewhere, nowhere to be seen.

Ludo holds me gently to him, "Come on," he says, "I've left the jeep round the corner". I follow him whilst looking around, knowing that if anyone sees us it will soon become gossip all over the village. We sit without talking as he drives down the country road.

"Where are we going?" I quietly ask him.

He gently places his hand over mine and says, "I don't know Elizabeth but I had to see you". He takes his hand off mine to turn the wheel and we pull into the woods. He kills the engine when he comes to a small clearing where we can't be seen from the road. He turns to me and holds out his arms, I lean straight into them, it feels so right and I want to stay in them forever.

"Elizabeth," he says.

I put my fingers to his lips, "We haven't much time Ludo. They'll be waiting for me up at the farm". I so want to be with him but know this is not the time.

"I know", he replies, "We are OK for a short time. I've talked to Maggie, she's at the farm and has made arrangements for you and her to be working in the yard all day".

All the worry and frustration I've been feeling hits me and I start to cry. I feel so foolish but Ludo just holds me quietly until I'm all cried out. Laughing quietly, he pulls out a large clean handkerchief, , "Here, I think you need this". I wipe my face, blow my nose and through my swollen eyes realise his shirt has a large wet patch on it. I try to dab it dry.

He holds my hand still, "Elizabeth, stop. I'm going to keep this shirt. When I fly again, it will be part of you with me forever".

I fill up again, "What are we going to do?". I feel like a young stupid girl.

He gently wipes my face, "Sweetheart, we are going to the farm and I am leaving you with your lovely friend Maggie".

He makes me laugh, "I know that! You know what I'm talking about".

He says, "Please come to me tonight, we must talk. No one will know you are there. I promise I won't take advantage of you". I think, *if only he knew how much I want him*. If he tried to take me now, I would not be able to stop him. He backs out of the cutting and we drive to the farm. I leave him at the gate but not without kissing him first, telling him, "I won't be able to come until sometime after eight. I'll have to work late to catch up; Maggie has probably done half my work now. I am so lucky to have such a great friend".

He gives one me of his wonderful smile, "Just come when you

can, I'll be waiting".

I open the farmhouse door and walk through it. I just love its warm welcome and the smell of bacon cooking makes me realise how hungry I am. I haven't eaten since my dinner on Sunday. Maggie has a fresh pot of tea ready. She is making me a bacon sandwich. I sit down and she puts the tea and sandwich onto the table. Then she leans down and grabs me in one of her bear hugs. She holds me so tight and I'm breathless. I stand up and hug her back, I am so glad she is there.

She pushes me away, looks at me and says, "Don't know what he sees in you kid, you look like shit".

She makes me laugh and I tell her. "Maggie I'm so glad to see you".

Then she looks as if she is going to cry and grabs me again. When she lets me go, I stagger a little. She shoves me down on the chair and pushes the tea and sandwich in front of me.

I go to speak, "Maggie---", I begin.

She shushes me. "Tell me in a minute Liz. You look terrible. Now drink your tea and eat your sandwich before you pass out. You can tell me everything when you've finished".

I sit quietly, drinking my tea and relishing eating my sandwich, taking in the warmth and smell of the kitchen. A feeling of peace creeps over me and I almost nod off. Maggie just goes about her business, making butter. As she turns the handle of the huge churn, everything seems back to normal. But of course it isn't and now I've finished the eating and drinking, I have to rouse myself. I know I have to face things again. Maggie stops turning the handle, comes over and pours herself a cup of tea then sits at the table facing me.

I stretch my hand out to her and she gets hold of it, "What would I do without you Maggie?" Maggie doesn't often look serious but as we hold hands, she talks to me.

"You look terrible Liz. Has something bad happened?"

"I've fallen in love and I shouldn't have. It's all I can think about, I know it's wrong". I moan and know I'm crying again. "Oh Maggie, I already love him more than I thought I could love anyone. I think about him day and night and we haven't even made love yet". I wail, "Maggie, what can I do?"

Maggie comes over to me and puts her hands on my shoulders. "Love, I've already told you to go with it. After all, there is a war on and none of know what is going to happen to us next".

Little did I know how true - what Maggie was saying to me - was going to be.

That night, I set off walking to meet Ludo at his house. I didn't want him to pick me up from the farm in case someone noticed. Maggie says she will cover for me if anyone asks where I am. What excuse she will manage to come up with, I'm not sure but I know she will work something out.

When we finish work, I eat my evening meal with the girls. They all ask how my day off went, I lie and say it was great. I listen to them talking about their day off and think to myself how uncomplicated they sound. Of course, one of them could be thinking the same about mine! I make an excuse as soon as I finish eating, saying I need an early night. Luckily I only share with Maggie. When I get to our room, I pour cold water out of the jug into the basin. I have realised if I were to take a kettle of hot water up to the room so early, someone would ask questions. I dress with care and put some of my treasured Californian Poppy perfume on. Then I sit waiting for Maggie to tell me when the coast is clear. What will I do without her?

CHAPTER ELEVEN:
FOREVER

I've been back at home in Barrow for quite some time now. The war has just ended so Fred will be de-mobbed at some point in the near future, how that future will work out, I'm not sure. I'm just living one day at a time, I can't even begin to imagine my life going back to what it was before the war. How things have changed since Ludo met me at the train station. I went to meet him that night as arranged and since then, I have had the most wonderful and the most heart-breaking times of my life. I think back to that night. I'd set off walking to meet Ludo at his house. I didn't want him to pick me up at the farm as word soon gets around the village here. It's a great place for gossip and several of the girls have been caught in the wrong place with the wrong person!

Some of the girls and GIs just had a good time while they could but others became engaged to their American sweethearts. Their men planned to marry them here and send for them as soon as they could, the plan being for their brides to move to America after the war. I don't think I would be brave enough to leave everything here for a foreign home. Another girl fell madly in love with her GI and left to have their baby but he let her down; turned out he was already married and had never intended to stay with her. Her family will probably send her to a mother and baby home for a few months, they won't want her home when she starts showing. She will have the baby taken away and put up for adoption almost immediately, then never ever be allowed to see it again or even talk about it to friends or family.

I'm married and know what I'm doing is wrong. Maggie has said she will cover for me if anyone asks where I am. What excuse she'll make up I have no idea, but I'm sure she'll work something out.

When I arrive at the lodge, the door is slightly open. I tap and wonder *should I walk in?* I feel as embarrassed and nervous as I did when I was a young girl on my first date with Fred. As I dither on the step, the door opens and Ludo smiles at me. He draws me through the open door into his arms, closing it gently behind me. I feel as if I'm standing outside of myself watching everything happen in slow motion. I think *this is it!* If I stay here now, I'm making a decision that will change my life. I am afraid, excited and very scared. Still, I feel so safe, loved and wanted in his arms. I suddenly know what I'm going to do.

Ludo leads me into his sitting room. A quick glance around shows me this place is almost identical to Miss Anderson's lodge on my quick visit to collect our Tom from the farm that day. It's very old fashioned but comfortably furnished. He sits me down on a well-worn but comfortable sofa. I sit straight up with my hands clasped on my knees and my back rigid, my feet don't quite touch the floor. He just smiles, signals then leaves me going into what must be the kitchen. When he comes back into the room, he's carrying a tray with two wine glasses and a decanter of what I think is red wine. He places it onto a small table next to the settee.

Then he asks me, "Would you like a glass of wine while we talk Elizabeth?" I don't like to tell him I've never tasted red wine. The only alcoholic drink I have had is a small glass of sherry at Christmas.

I don't want to seem ignorant or unsophisticated so I nod, "Just a tiny one please. I don't really drink much wine".

He seems to think I want something else. He says, "Sorry I should have asked, I have gin or whisky if you want it?"

I shudder at the thought and say, "Oh no! I don't like either of those". It flits through my mind the only time I drank a bottle of gin was when I was pregnant with Jane. I had such a bad hangover and was so sick I don't even like to hear the word *gin* mentioned. While I was thinking about this, Ludo stands looking at me.

Then he smiles, "Would you rather I made us a cup of tea, Elizabeth?"

I'm so relieved and nod, "Yes please". He goes back into the kitchen and I hear china rattling. He comes back through the door carrying a pretty tray with a china teapot, sugar dish, milk jug and two cups and saucers to match.

I'm surprised, "That was quick, are you having tea? What about the wine?"

He pours the tea and says, "I would rather have tea too. It was just me thinking it would be a romantic gesture to offer you wine. So far I haven't had chance to show you how romantic I can be". We both laugh and I relax a little as he passes me my tea.

I say, "Oh so you usually make romantic gestures". I'm sorry I've said it because he looks so embarrassed. "I was only joking Ludo", I say seriously, "I know what we have is special and you feel the same as I do".

He takes my tea from me then draws me towards him. "Elizabeth, I love you so much it hurts every time I think about you - and that's all the time".

I tell him, "I have a confession to make. I'm not like you, I've never tasted red wine in my life. I'm a working class girl and people in my life usually drink beer. Or Guinness".

He shakes his head and kisses me gently on my lips. "Sweet-heart, I would not like you to be any different. To me you are the most wonderful and beautiful girl". He stops smiling and looks very serious. "I love you so much. Yes I'm younger than you are and I have met a few other girls. However this is different. I don't think I could ever be happy again if you were to say you don't love me".

My heart pounds, I know I'm going to cry again as I'm feeling so emotional. I lean away from him and say, "Let's not talk about anything just now".

He just says, "OK" and walks away from me. I'm not sure what to do, should I sit back down or remain standing where I am? He has his back to me, faffing with something at the sideboard. I realise he has a gramophone record in his hand. He puts the record onto his gramophone. Glen Miller, my favourite orchestra, starts to play *Perphidia*. My first thought is about the day I married Fred. I start to panic. Then he holds his hands out to me. I feel his arms around me and all my fears just dissolve. I think that I might never have this wonderful chance ever again. We start to have our first really romantic dance together. Not moving much, we just sway together to the music. We kiss and look into each other's eyes. I see the passion as he looks at me and I lose my breath again. He leans into my neck and kisses it. I fight to hold back my feelings, I need him so much. The first tune stops and he signals to me to wait as he puts another record on. The song *At Last* starts to play and I think to myself, *these words are meant just for us.* I can feel Ludo is longing to take it further, and so am I. I sink into his body and as we sway to the music, I feel as if we are molded together. A great feeling of security steals over me. I know this man will never intentionally let me down and I want him in my future. But that is for later. All I want now is for him to fully take my body.

As if he is reading my mind, he sweeps me up into his arms and carries me into his bedroom. He places me very gently onto his bed then stands and stares at me. I stare back at him knowing I'm showing my love for him in my eyes. "What are we going to do Ludo?"

He knows what I mean. He sits on the bed, lifts me into his arms and cradles me. "Right now I just want to make love to you Elizabeth". Then he falters, "That is, if you feel the same way".

I'm now so breathless because of the need to be with him and I can't answer. I take a very deep breath, "Oh Ludo, I do feel the way you do. Please", I moan.

If he knew what I was feeling, thinking, wanting, I would be totally embarrassed. I start to unbutton his shirt. He lays me back onto the bed and removes his shirt. I gasp as I see his wonderful body. Then he lifts my blouse over my shoulders and removes it. He pulls me tight to his chest and we lay together. I feel the warmth of his bare chest on mine. I move, lay my head onto his chest and am aware of every beat of his heart. He starts to gently undress the rest of me and we make love for the first time. It is everything that I have dreamed about these past few weeks.

Afterwards I relax, feeling that this is where I should be. We don't talk for some time. Ludo lies back with his arm under my head as I lean on his shoulder. He smokes a cigarette. I have seen him smoking when he was driving but this feels so familiar, as if we are a real couple. We don't need to talk though I know we have to, but not now. I just want to enjoy this happy and peaceful feeling. There has been so much stress in my life these last few months, this sense of peace feels wonderful. We have to make some hard decisions soon, but not tonight. I close my eyes feeling Ludo stroke my hair. I open them and he is looking at me wit,h a right soft look on his face. I giggle and tell him, "Ludo I feel like a daft kid! Everything that is happening to me makes me feel about 17!

He catches my hand and kisses it, "Sweetheart, you will always be 17 to me, even when we grow old together. I want to spend the rest of my life loving and taking care of you". He pleads with me...

"Please tell me you'll love and stay with me for the rest of my life?"

I know I cannot promise that, not yet. "I love you, will always, and forever". I reply, kissing him passionately.

He responds as I knew he would, and I feel a passion rising in me that I have never felt before. We make love again and it is heaven. He kisses my eyes, lips, neck then my breasts. He strokes and explores every part of my body. I realise I am encountering new heights and feelings that I've never experienced before. I hold him as close as I can, want him to swallow me up, engulf me, so that we are never parted. Then I feel as if fireworks are exploding through my body, I never want it to stop. But it does and I fall back into his arms. This time we lay together in total exhaustion. I am so content. I think about my feelings for him and know I can't ignore them.

We both go quiet and I look at my love, Ludo, who's sound asleep. I stare at his sweet handsome face. He hasn't a single line to show what he's already been through in this war. I think about the last two or three years he's been flying. He's been in the most dangerous of situations as a rear gunner. I feel sad and afraid, the life expectation of all young airman are almost zero, and I've fallen so much in love with this man. I feel tears on my face again and wonder *what I am doing?* I lean over and gently kiss his precious mouth. He stirs and opens his eyes, smiles at me then goes straight back to sleep. I realise I must get some rest also. I think if only this night could go on forever I would be happy.

I wake with a start, it's 5 o'clock and I should be back at the farm already. I turn over expecting to see Ludo lying next to me but I'm surprised he isn't here. I sit up to get out of bed as Ludo walks through the bedroom door carrying a cup of tea for me.

I'm confused, "You're dressed! How long have you been up?"

"Only about half an hour, Elizabeth. You were fast asleep and looked so sweet that I did not want to disturb you. I know you need to be back at the farm soon, drink your tea as you get dressed".

I pull myself up off the pillow, lean back and sip the tea he has passed to me. He is standing by the bed looking at me. I feel embarrassed and can't imagine how I must look to him right now. I put my cup down and try to straighten my hair. I say, "Stop staring at me Ludo, I must look awful". He is still looking down at me so I ask him, "What are you looking at me for? Please go away so I can get up and dressed. I have nothing on under this sheet".

He picks me up into his arms, still with the sheet wrapped around me and laughs. "Elizabeth, how can you even try to be shy with me after last night?"

I realise I would be silly to try to be coy so I kiss him and say, "I love you so much Ludo". He kisses me back, gently then passionately.

I push him away, "Stop, stop, I have to get dressed," I tell him, "Put me down, I'll be late, the farm!"

He puts me down gently as if I was a delicate piece of China. "I know," he says. He laughs again and gently slaps me over the sheet on my bottom. Says, "Come on sweetheart, you've a job to go to. If you stand about half naked in front of me like this, I have to tell you that you will be very late".

I laugh and say, "Get out of the bedroom now and let me get dressed".

This time I need him to drop me off at the farm, I just hope no one sees us. Luckily there's no one about when we arrive at the gate so we kiss. Ludo holds me tight and says, "Tonight".

I nod, "I'll walk up about the same time as last night". Then I get out of the jeep and walk very fast up the yard, hoping no one is down yet.

As I sneak through the farmhouse door, I realise the lamp is lit. Maggie is there and she signals to me to go up to our bedroom to change. I know the girls would soon realise what I was up to if they saw how I was dressed so I quickly dash upstairs to change. I pour the jug of cold water into the bowl and wash my face as I think about last night. I know whatever happens in the future, I will love Ludo for the rest of my life.

As I walk back down the stairs, I'm hoping the girls haven't noticed I was missing last night. As soon as I walk into the kitchen, they start asking me if I feel better. I flash a look at Maggie. "I told everyone that you were feeling tired out and under the weather so I made you go to bed". As everyone turns to look at me, she winks and grins. "I thought the night in bed would do you the world of good. Not sure it has though, you look as if you've been up all night, girl".

I bluster, "Maggie, I have had a really good rest and feel fine".

"Well kid, lucky you and me have to clean the pigs out again so we're here today, and there'll be no skiving seeing that you've had such a restful night". She puts her eyes up at me again.

I can't help but smile at her mischievous look, "OK I'm ready to start work, put me in with the pigs when you're ready". By now the others have left the table. They're all picking up their lunch baskets and leaving, shouting their goodbyes as they go out of the door. I just love Maggie, she's such a friend. I would never have got through the day out in the fields.

CHAPTER TWELVE:
QUESTION

It's haymaking time and we've to work until dusk as the farmers need to take advantage of the good weather. Everything we do on the farm is so important to the war effort. We might not build ships or airplanes or armaments, but the production of food is of utmost importance. There is such a shortage of most things, and wheat and potatoes are our lifeline. As are meat, milk and eggs which we get very little of in our rations. Wheat or potatoes go into almost every article of food us ordinary women cook to try and make things go further. I really shouldn't moan to myself about shortages because at the farm, we really do have the best of food. Our boss - for all his faults - is never mean with extra rations. Like the odd pig hanging hidden away in the shed. We're never short of bacon with our eggs and always have fresh butter on our bread.

As soon as the last of the girls leave, Maggie comes over to me, grabs me in one of her hugs then pushes me back and has a good look at me.

She says, "I've missed you girl, tea's made so sit down at the table and tell me all".

I pick up my tea, drinking large mouthful, then pick up a piece of the toast and take a large bite. I'm so hungry I eat and drink with relish. Maggie laughs at me then gets up and makes me more toast. When she puts it in front of me, she sits down and says, "Right kid, spill the beans".

I swallow another mouthful of tea and tell her, "Oh Maggie, he loves me, really loves me".

"Loves you? I would never have guessed. After all, he's only been lost and miserable all weekend, I've seen him so many times. The others have started to think it's me that's having a fling with him".

"Why?" I ask her, "What has he been doing?"

"Well, wherever I've been working, he just happens to have been passing and has stopped to have a word with me. Always asking if I've heard from you, the lad is mad about you. Now you've finally---", she hesitates and laughs, "---you know what? How was it?"

I'm shocked, "Maggie! What a question!". I'm embarrassed but *have* to tell her. "It was wonderful, everything I could have hoped for and more. You were right, he is a man *not* a boy and he is so serious about this, he wants us to spend the rest of our lives together".

Maggie smiles and holds my hand, "That's OK then isn't it?"

I repeat her "OK", suddenly realising everything is not going to be OK. I feel terrible, a great sense of doom flows over me.

"Oh Maggie, what have I done? I've never felt like this before, it's all consuming. What am I going to do?". I start wailing. Then think to myself, *woman it's time you grew up*, though it doesn't change how I feel. Maggie just sits there eating her toast. "What would you do if you were me?" I ask.

She sits quietly munching her toast, obviously thinking. "Look, love", she says, "any other time, I wouldn't be able to say this. Times are hard and no one knows what's going to happen in the near future. So I would say, enjoy what you have while you can. If it is meant to be, it will be. This is the only bit of advice I'm giving you. I know I wouldn't be able to turn the love he has for you down". She just shrugs and I know what she means.

Ludo and me continue to see each other every night for the next two weeks. He even drives me home to Barrow on the Saturday nights and books into a little bed and breakfast place nearby. He comes to my house very late at night and stays with me until early morning, leaving before the kids wake up. I carry on as normal and have my usual Sunday dinner with the kids at Mother and Dad's house. I do feel awful about leaving Ludo alone on the Sunday but luckily he's found a Servicemen's Club. He tells me that volunteers from the Catholic Women's League run it through their church, and they feed him very well. In fact, several have invited him to visit their homes. I know most of the women have daughters at home and I'm

111 of the women have daughters at home and I'm

afraid Ludo will meet a prettier, younger girl. I tell him if he does, he should move on from me. It would break my heart if he did but then again, it would be all I deserve. He gets really mad at me and tells me he has never loved anyone the way he loves me. He makes me the happiest woman in the world. Now all I want with him is forever and forever.

Monday morning always comes too soon. He leaves half an hour before the kids get up then picks me up at the railway station gates after I've dropped them off at Mother's house. I have never felt so alive, or so afraid. Having him with me is wonderful.

Mother knows I'm telling the truth about how busy it is on the farm. When she was at the pictures, she'd seen a feature on Pathé News about how hard and what long hours we 'land girls' are working. They had shown how busy we are with the haymaking. They say on the film that we are 'unsung heroes'. I think Mam feels slightly guilty but knows Dad has decided I've to come home and that's that. Now I have to leave the farm because the harvest is in and Dad has told me he won't take any more excuses.

So I am leaving the farm this next weekend. I am going to miss my best friend Maggie so much! We promise each other we are always going to keep in touch and except for leaving Maggie, I actually don't mind not staying longer at the farm. Ludo isn't at the Lodge anymore. He was called back to see his surgeon who declared him fit to return to his unit. Luckily we've had those two wonderful weeks together and have decided we are meant for each other. He came to see me as soon as he could after seeing his surgeon. He told me he was happy to be returning to his group but I felt as if he was deserting me. Then he told me why he was happy and I know him enough to accept how he is feeling. He felt he would be back again with his comrades helping them to win this terrible war. Although he is going back now, he still has six weeks before he can fly with his unit again. He is being allowed to have every weekend off until then, and is only just over an hour and a half away from me on the train.

This last six weeks, Ludo and I have spent every minute that we can together. It's now a month since I left the farm and he starts flying again in two weeks. These few weeks have been marvelous apart from the guilt but when I'm with Ludo it soon disappears. I've had a brainwave and decide to turn the parlour into a private place for Ludo and me. It's been left as it was since Mr Brown left. Although the bed is only a single, I know we will happily share it. I haven't actually unlocked the parlour door yet because I haven't had time to clean it, so the kids are used to not going into it. Now it means we can keep the door locked and we will have 'our place'.

I work like mad, cleaning and shining everything in it and make a pretty new rag rug to place in front of the bed. I also put some pretty chintz curtains up over the ugly blackout blinds and two cushions to brighten the bed. They cost me my fox fur, one of our Bella's friends had always wanted it. Bella knows her friend had some pretty chintz material given to her from her gran, and she'd planned to make a dress but wasn't much of a seamstress. Bella told me about the material so I offered to buy it. All she wanted for it she said, was my fox fur and as I hadn't worn it for some time now, it was great exchange.

I can now make a meal for us to sit and eat at the little occasional table I had previously kept upstairs. Then, with a fire burning in the grate, it feels as if we will be together like this forever. I clean the wall cupboards out and keep anything personal that belongs to Ludo in there. It becomes our very own special place and means the world to me. It also means Jane can sleep in my bed which she loves and sleeps very easy in it. She's never settled down as quickly as Tom and is very nosey if she hears voices, shouting down, *who's there?* Now she sleeps right through the night.

Tonight I get the kids to bed as early as I can. Ludo is coming and I want to make myself look nice for him. I've made his favourite meal of meat and potato pie as I'd managed to get half a pound of best mince from Mr Parker, our local butcher, and an onion at Pearson's Fruit and Veg' shop. I've also made apple and rhubarb pie. The kids will think all their boats have come in when they get some for their tea tomorrow. There's a knock at the door and someone walks up the lobby. I know it's not Ludo as it's too early and the footsteps are heavy and fast. I realise it's Mrs Carr. She rushes through the door and plonks her large body down on a chair at the kitchen table. I look at her, wondering why she's called in so late.

"Hiya", I say. "This is an unexpected visit. Are the kids all in bed?" I look at the clock and realise I've plenty of time so put tea in the pot. "Cuppa?" I wave a cup towards her.

She nods. "Yes I've got time, the two big 'uns are listening to *It's That Man Again* on the radio". Then she looks annoyed. "Want to ask you something". I pour the tea now it's mashed and I think *Uh-oh, what now?* We drink our tea and I wait until she's ready.

She says, "I'm your best friend so I'm going to come right out with it. Are you having an affair?"

I am shocked! I thought Ludo and I had been so careful. I'm embarrassed because even though she is one of my best friends, this is the one thing I haven't been truthful to her about. I hesitate then decide it's time to come clean. "I'm sorry Mrs Carr", thinking to myself *where do I start?* I then admit it, "Yes. But how do you know?"

She shakes her head, "'Lizbeth, you should know nothing gets past the neighbours round here". She points at the chair facing her. "Right, you'd better sit down and put me in the picture hadn't you? I've even heard he stays here".

I need to sit down as my legs are shaking, "How did you find out?" I ask.

"Mr Harrison, the Grocer from up the street, saw him leaving at 5 o'clock in the morning last week. Before you ask, he had to go into work early to get his points ready to send off". I know I'm in real trouble. If you want to know any gossip around here, there's always a customer in the Grocer's queue who'll put you in the picture.

"Oh my God, is it everywhere?" I ask in horror.

"No 'Lizbeth, luckily it isn't. He likes you and hasn't told anyone except me. I told him it was probably one of Fred's brothers from Liverpool on leave. I said they sometime come overnight and have to get the early train back".

Before I answer, she says, "Don't tell me anything but the truth 'Lizbeth".

I answer her in tears, mainly because I know I should have trusted her. "I'm so sorry, it's a long story. Have you time for me to tell you what's happened?"

She's such a kind friend and she hugs me, "Aye lass, just start at the beginning".

When I finish telling her everything that's happened I realise what a good friend she is. Standing up, she hugs me and says, "Who am I to judge you 'Lizbeth? He sounds a nice man and a brave one from what you say, but it will all end in tears you know. The only thing I can advise you is to be more discreet, think about your kids. I'll have to go now, *ITMA* has finished".

As she leaves, I ask, "Would you like to meet him? He's coming here tonight".

She shakes her head, "No 'Lizbeth, I can't. I understand how you feel but I can't condone it". I start to cry again as she leaves, suddenly feeling very lonely. I look at the clock and it's half an hour after Ludo should have been here. I sit up waiting all night for Ludo to arrive but there's no sign.

The next morning I'm frantic with worry but know I have to get the kids up and myself to work. I go through the motions, even calling at Mother's house for a cup of tea as usual when I've finished my rounds. She knows there's something wrong but I can't possibly tell her. I just say I'm having women's trouble and she leaves it at that, although she looks at me funny.

She says, "Look, go home and have a rest, I'll send Dad to get the kids from school. We'll bring them back home about seven".

"Thanks Mother, I don't know what I'd do without you". I'm relieved and need to think. I have the most dreadful feeling in my stomach. I know Ludo can't have been shot down as he hasn't actually started flying yet. So I think to myself, *stop worrying*. I will wait until tonight, he should turn up or get in touch with me by then.

There's a knock at the door and I glance up, the clock says 9. I realise it's quite dark outside and I haven't even noticed. I've just been sitting here, quietly waiting. I rush to open the door, just knowing it isn't Ludo. He knows the door is always open for him. It's late so I open it very carefully and gasp, almost passing out, as I see two strangers standing there. They are both wearing Air Force uniforms. Then I realise that I do know one of them. It's Lotto, Ludo's friend. I met him once when Ludo was living at the Lodge. He was another very nice young Polish airman. He gets hold of my hand and asks in a much heavier Polish accent than Ludo, "Can we come in, Elizabeth?"

I nod and lead them up the lobby. "It's not Ludo?" I plead, "It can't be, he's not flying yet".

Lotto says, "Sit down Elizabeth, we have to talk". He leads me to the chair I just left to answer the door. I do as I'm told and they both sit across from me. I notice the one I don't know is older, wearing a different uniform to Lotto. I think to myself, *they don't have to tell me, I know, I can feel it!* Still, I realise they have to tell me but I think if I don't let them say it out loud, it won't be true. It cannot be true, he hasn't started flying yet. I hear the older airman talking. He's saying something to me about lorries and trains. I look at him and shake my head, Ludo should be here. Lotto brings me a glass of water, holds my hand and says, "It's true Elizabeth. Last night he was on the train coming here. An army lorry ploughed through the safety barriers at a crossing. Three soldiers were killed in the lorry and Ludo was killed on the train".

"On the train?" I'm confused. "No, there's no way, there are no air raids now. What was the lorry there for?"

Lotto tells me, "Elizabeth, it was a freak accident, the lorry's brakes failed. It was lucky more weren't killed as the lorry was full of soldiers transferring to another station".

I know I am being punished, "It's my fault, my Ludo, killed. If I hadn't have loved him, he would still be here".

They ask if I have someone to come to sit with me. I want Maggie but she isn't here. Though it's late, I know Mrs Carr won't have gone to bed yet as she likes to sit up for a couple of hours after the kids and her husband have gone to bed. I think it's the only time she has some peace. I know I need someone and she will help me.

I nod and point to next door's wall, "Mrs Carr, she's still up. Please knock quietly, she'll come in".

Lotto goes up the lobby and less than a minute later, he returns with Mrs Carr in tow. They get up to leave as soon as she puts her arms around me. Lotto leans down to give me a kiss on my cheek, saying. "I'm so sorry. Elizabeth, whatever happens now, please know you made Ludo's last year full and happy. I hope you have a good future". The older man adds, "I'm sorry we have had to break such bad news, Elizabeth. Ludo told me so much about you. He was one of the nicest young men in our unit and after meeting you, the happiest man I've known. At least you both knew happier times before he died". They leave and I sob into my friend Mrs Carr's chest. She sits with me for most of the night and lets me talk and talk. Finally I'm exhausted and realise how tired she must be. I get up make a cup of tea and pass one to her. We sit drinking it without speaking.

The she says, "Go to bed now love, try to get some rest. You have to look after the kids. Ludo's dead. Your life will have to go on as if everything is normal now 'Lizbeth".

I stupidly say, "No, no, I don't believe you. He couldn't be killed on a train". I stop and shake my head, telling her, "It's a ridiculous thing to say to me".

She just holds me while I cry, then looks at me with sadness in her eyes. She hugs me again and leaves. It is true, I have lost him. Forever. I want to die. But I can't, I have to carry on.

CHAPTER THIRTEEN:
VICTORY

I have survived. The war has ended. Life carries on and I decide to make the best of what I've got. Fred isn't home yet but it won't be long. I know already that the gossips can't wait.

This past year I've worked two jobs as well as having the kids to take care of so have kept very busy. I've even managed to take them on a week's holiday to Biddston in Cheshire to my Aunty Florrie's cottage. It was really good for me. We fed the hens and the horses, and went for long walks through the countryside. Tom did have a near fatal accident though by slipping into a stinking slurry pool. He hollered so loud that the farmer heard him and pulled him out before he went under. I had to hose him down in the garden before pulling the tin bath onto the lawn and making him having a bath outside. It put my life into perspective.

When we arrived home, the kids flew off to tell their friends about their holiday and I immediately unlocked and opened the parlour door. I hadn't been inside since the night Ludo had died. That night, after Mrs Carr went home, I had laid myself down on the bed and held the sweater that Ludo had left, his other items in the cupboards. I had held it to my nose and smelt his essence that had lingered in the fabric and said my goodbyes. Then I slept fitfully and dreamt he was still with me. But when I woke the following morning listening to the kids bickering, I knew he had gone forever. Now I pick up the sweater from the bed where it has lain ever since and put it to my nose to smell it. All I smell now is the damp musky smell of an empty, neglected room. Ludo has gone and I have finally accepted it.

I open the blinds, pull off the bedding and take the rug to the back door to shake off the soot that had settled onto it from the empty fireplace. For two days, I washed and cleaned everything in that room. The morning after, I ushered both kids into it and said, "Look, we have a lovely bright new parlour". They loved it, Jane especially and she fussed as usual. I got mad with her and realised that I had moved on.

Although I would *never* ever forget my dearest love, my Ludo, my life and those around me needed my attention.

It seems funny that although we all think we're starting to win the war, this year - 1944 – our government has banned all foreign travel. Not that I know anyone who has ever been abroad. Who would want to have a holiday in places where you couldn't speak the language? The only ones we hear of who've ever travelled 'other than in the services' are the King and Queen, or posh knobs like Lords and Ladies who're rolling in money.

I don't go out often anymore but our Bella and her friends come over for drinks sometimes of an evening. I have told her everything about Ludo and what has happened. She has been good at keeping my spirits up. We have lot of laughs and the drink flows. I have also found out plenty of drink wipes out most of my memories when I go to bed.

I've made a decision like many other married women have had to - I am going to try to make my life with Fred work. However, I am not the 'little woman' anymore and want to carry on working. After all, it's now the summer of '45. We have had a general election and just voted Mr Attlee in as our Labour Prime Minister. It was an overwhelming win, mainly because the returning servicemen had lost faith in Mr Churchill and the last Tory government.

Everything is going to change. For the best, I hope!

I've decided I am going to open a Greengrocer's shop when Fred is discharged. I know he won't be happy about it but compared to some of the problems we'll face, I think it's one argument I will win. I'm not sure about how the future will go but I do know it will be different and am pretty sure Fred won't like it. I am a completely different woman to the one he left behind.

CHAPTER FOURTEEN:
AFTERWORD

The difficulty in targeting Barrow's shipyard by the German Luftwaffe meant that many of the residential neighbourhoods were (intentionally or accidentally, you pick!) bombed instead: 83 civilians were killed, 330 injured and over 10000 houses damaged or destroyed during the so-called Barrow Blitz, about 25% of the town's housing stock.

Many surrounding towns and villages were often mistaken for Barrow and attacked, and many streets in Barrow were severely damaged. Bombing during mid-April 1941 caused significant damage to the central portion of Abbey Road, destroying the *Waverley Hotel* as well as the *Christ Church* and the *Baptist Church*. The town's main public swimming baths and the *Gaiety Theatre* were also severely damaged, though repaired within a few years. Hawcoat Lane was a street that took a direct destructive hit in early May 1941.

Barrow has been described as somewhat unprepared for the Blitz as there were only enough public shelters for just 5% of the population, resulting in some people from in the town centre being forced to seek refuge in hedgerows on the outskirts of Barrow. This shortage of shelters was believed to have led to the excessively high casualties.

The headquarters of Barrow's anti-aircraft defences were located at the *Furness Abbey Hotel*, situated towards the outskirts of the town (a wing of which is now the modern *Abbey Tavern* public house, though closed in recent years). It was a huge sandstone building located in a valley screened by trees, next to a small railway station adjacent to the old ruins of a 12th century Abbey. One would think it would have been an unlikely target; nevertheless, it was attacked and badly damaged by the Luftwaffe in May 1941.

Barrow's Victorian railway station was also heavily damaged on 7th May 1941. To this day, a WWI memorial located within it still bears the holes and gashes caused by the WWII bombings.

Source: Wikipedia

TIMELINE:

Sep 1940:   First compulsory blackout in Barrow.

300 incendiary bombs dropped on Salthouse, Barrow.

5-year-old child becomes first victim of the Barrow Blitz.

Apr 1941:   Central section of Abbey Road is significantly bombed.

May 1941:   Bombing intensifies with landmines, incendiaries and high explosives dropped.

Anti-aircraft defences stationed at *Furness Abbey Hotel* are attacked and badly damaged

Barrow's Victorian railway station is completely destroyed by bombing.

Two firewatchers are killed when the hammerhead crane they were stationed in at the shipyard is bombed.

Some 2,250 children are evacuated.

Jun 1941:   A further 4000 children are also evacuated as the death toll from bombing exceeds 80.

Jan 1942:   The last bombs are dropped on Barrow with no recorded casualties.

Mar 1942:   Last air-raid siren in Barrow was recorded on 25 Mar 1942.

Source: Wikipedia

APPENDIX A:
FURTHER PHOTOS

Figure 17 – Aerial Shot of Barrow Paper Mill (Closed 1976)
(Where Fred worked full-time prior to enlisting for the army)

Figure 18 - Inside the Local Laundry, c1950
(Where I was employed prior to marrying Fred, after being sacked from my first job at the 'big house' for stealing bread).

Figure 19 - Barrow Park Steps Leading to the Bandstand
(Where I shyly spoke to Fred for the first time on our unofficial 'first date')

Figure 20 - Bombed Out Houses Following the Blitz, 1941

Figure 21 – Waverley Hotel, Abbey Road

(Destroyed during the Barrow Blitz of 1941, the site is now the *Coronation Gardens*, now adjacent to Barrow Magistrates' Court, itself formerly the site of the public Abbey Baths).

Figure 22 – Baptist Church, Abbey Road
(Destroyed during the Barrow Blitz of 1941).

Figure 24 – Abbey Baths, Heavily Bombed During the Blitz
(Low-resolution, slightly blurred image showing bomb damage. Abbey
Baths went on to be repaired, but was finally demolished in the early 1990s
to make way for the new Magistrates' Courts. It is next to the *Coronation
Gardens* opposite the offices currently occupied by the *North West Evening
Mail* local newspaper).

Figure 25 - Christ Church, Destroyed During the Blitz

Figure 26 - Hawcoat Lane, Heavily Devastated by the Blitz

ABOUT THE AUTHOR

Hi, I'm Lilian.   I was born in 1936 and live on Walney Island next to a small peninsular in the North-West of England, part of the Barrow-in-Furness district in Cumbria, then part of Lancashire. Barrow is a working class shipyard town of some 70,000 inhabitants, and was involved with the building of submarines, surface ships, large guns, and other armaments etc for and during WWII.

I have always lived with lots of stories in my head.   On retirement, I took an A and B course in Creative Writing through Lancaster University.   I went on to do more Creative Writing and Moving On courses, also writing for radio.   I wrote a comedy play, which was produced for the local theatre, and have had several articles published in magazines and local newspapers, as well as short stories and poetry.

I used the initial chapter of the first book in this *'Cos That's The Way...* series to enter a screenwriting competition aimed at Cumbrian women.   I became one of ten finalists and was 30 years older than the other contestants!   The chapter won me my place, and Jane's wartime story came to be published as a paperback, later in digital format on Amazon Kindle.   In contrast and to complement *this* book (second in the series), the former is an eye view account of working class life from the perspective of a little girl, called Jane, during WWII in roughly the same time frame.

Both these books have now been received into the Barrow

Library Archives, local museums and historic visitor attractions. It has sold almost 1500 copies. Now I am regularly invited to groups and schools to give talks about my life as a wartime child.

Unfortunately, I missed a lot of school through WWII and subsequent events, so life has been *my* teacher. I was evacuated from Barrow at five years old, enduring several moves due to neglect, death, overcrowding etc. In the end, I thought I was never to go home.

I was almost nine before I saw home again, and 10 (my older brother Tom was 13) when our father de-mobbed from the eighth army, returning home. But he was a complete stranger to me and I have always felt that although he didn't die during WWII, *I still lost my father.*

At 12, my mother began to train me in floristry, working in our small family business; it turned out to be the best thing she ever did for me as it opened many doors in my life, both here and abroad.

Mother eventually became an alcoholic and Father a drunk. They fought both physically and mentally from the moment he arrived home following the war, and it made life difficult for us all. Tom subsequently left home at 14 years old to live and work on a farm.

I have started writing the third part in the *'Cos That's The Way...* series which covers the next 10 years of Jane's story.

I love what I have done so far! I have had a hard but colourful long life with many experiences - some funny and others not so much. Still, I am tough and resilient. I don't give in easily and enjoy writing, updating my blog and commenting on day-to-day life around me and the world in general; I look forward to making you smile at some of my stories.

Find out more about me at www.wookeysworld.com.

North-Western

Evening Mail

FINAL

BARROW-IN-FURNESS, MONDAY, 30 APRIL, 1945   THREE HALFPENCE

Bernadotte Returning With Himmler's Final Answer

WORLD AWAITS NAZI SURRENDER
ANNOUNCEMENT

OVER-ALL PICTURE OF NAZI DISASTER

Hitler Is Dead— Reports Persist

SUPERFICIALLY the war situation remains unchanged except that in London informed opinion has hardened and there is no longer any doubt that armistice moves are in train and moving swiftly.

THE FORECAST OF LAST NIGHT THAT THE END MAY COME WITHIN A MATTER OF DAYS OR EVEN IN HOURS CONTINUES TO HAVE STRONG SUPPORT

Announcement To-morrow ?

Nearer To Rangoon

"Hitler Was Raving"

DIM-OUT AND LIGHTING UP TIME

GET HIMMLER: GERMANS TOLD

BRITISH DRIVE FOR BALTIC COAST

American Threat In Redoubt Area

WITH MUNICH ENTERED AND BERLIN FURTHER REDUCED BRITISH AND RUSSIAN FORCES ARE HEADING FOR A NEW NORTHERN LINK-UP

Skymen Drop Into Berlin Cauldron

BIG GAINS ALONG ITALIAN FRONT
Tito's Troops In Trieste

MORE HORRORS REVEALED AT DACHAU

CANADIANS NEW THRUST

Telephone Ban On Enemy Suggested